AF600640

RESERVATION OF CENSURES

THE CATHOLIC UNIVERSITY OF AMERICA
CANON LAW STUDIES
No. 208

Reservation of Censures

A COMMENTARY WITH HISTORICAL NOTES ON THE NATURE OF THE RESERVATION OF CENSURES

BY

REV. CASIMIR J. STADALNIKAS, M.I.C., J.C.L.
PRIEST OF THE CONGREGATION OF THE MARIAN FATHERS

A DISSERTATION

SUBMITTED TO THE FACULTY OF THE SCHOOL OF CANON LAW OF THE CATHOLIC UNIVERSITY OF AMERICA IN PARTIAL FULFILLMENT OF THE REQUIREMENTS FOR THE DEGREE OF DOCTOR OF CANON LAW

THE CATHOLIC UNIVERSITY OF AMERICA PRESS
WASHINGTON, D. C.
1944

NIHIL OBSTAT:

IOSEPHUS MACIULIONIS, M.I.C., J.C.L.,
ALPHONSUS JAGMINAS, M.I.C., PH.D., S.T.L.,
Censores Deputati.

IMPRIMI POTEST:

IOANNES JANCIUS, M.I.C., S.T.L.,
Superior Provincialis.
Chicagiae, Illinois, die 20 Iunii, 1944.

NIHIL OBSTAT:

HIERONYMUS D. HANNAN, S.T.D., J.C.D.,
Censor Deputatus.
Washingtonii, D. C., die VI Ianuarii, 1945.

IMPRIMATUR:

MICHAEL J. CURLEY, D.D.,
Archiepiscopus Baltimorensis-Washingtonensis.
Baltimorae, Md., die VI Ianuarii, 1945.

MURRAY & HEISTER
WASHINGTON, D. C.

PRINTED BY
TIMES AND NEWS PUBLISHING CO.
GETTYSBURG, PA., U. S. A.

INTRODUCTION

The purpose of the present work is to outline the main historical facts connected with the origin of the reservation of censures and to present a canonical commentary on canons 2245, 2246 and 2247, which deal with the reservation of censures. The reservation of sins alone and of vindicative penalties is beyond the proper scope of this dissertation. Matters relating to absolution from reserved censures and to special faculties in regard to reserved censures are introduced only to illustrate the binding force of reservation.

In the first chapter attention is given to the institute of reservation as it existed in the Decretals and as it was understood by contemporary authors. The effects of papal reservations upon the jurisdiction of both the bishop and the confessor as well as the effects of episcopal reservations upon the jurisdiction of the confessor constitute an important factor in determining the nature of reservation. Since many moralists treated of this question, especially after the Council of Trent, their opinions are advanced in order to present some of the difficulties which arose and the manner in which they were solved.

The development of the reservation of censures clearly portrays the incipient and spontaneous exercise of an innate right and duty of the Church and its governing ministers. The circumstances of the early Christian community did not call for the exercise of the power of the Pope and the bishops to reserve censures. With the growth of the Christian community the necessity to reserve censures to the judgment of more prudent ecclesiastical superiors became manifest.

In the canonical commentary the points under consideration are the following: in the second chapter the precise nature of reservation; in the third chapter the power of reservation with the different factors influencing that power, i.e., restrictions imposed by law in reference to higher authority, place and persons affected; in the fourth chapter the interpretation of a constituted reservation and the extension of the species of reserved censures; in the fifth chapter the special question of *latae sententiae* determined censures which are attached to particular precepts; and in the final chapter the effects of ignorance on the part of the confessor or the penitent upon the reservation of censures.

The writer wishes to take this occasion to acknowledge his sincere appreciation to his former Provincial, the Very Reverend Casimir Reklaitis, M.I.C., S.T.D., Ph.D., for the privilege of advanced study in Canon Law, and to his present Provincial, Very Reverend John J. Jancius, M.I.C., S.T.L., for the opportunity to complete his studies. He further wishes to express his deep gratitude to the Faculty of the School of Canon Law of the Catholic University of America for their considerate and generous assistance. In short, he wishes to give acknowledgment and thanks to all who have contributed in any way in the preparation of this dissertation.

TABLE OF CONTENTS

TABLE OF CONTENTS (Continued)

TABLE OF CONTENTS (Continued)

CHAPTER I

Reservation of Censures Before the Council of Trent

ARTICLE I. CENSURES RESERVED TO THE POPE

Papal reservation of censures originated in the practice of calling to Rome for absolution penitents who had incurred a specified excommunication. At first, then, absolution from the censure had to be obtained personally from the Pope. The term "reservation" was not applied to censures, but factual reservation was expressed by different phrases.[1] Many authors of the twelfth

---

[1] Pope Alexander III (1159-1181): ". . . pro sua absolutione debent ad Apostolicam sedem venire." ". . . a te vel ab alio quolibet sine speciali mandato Romani Pontificis absolvi non possint." ". . . donec . . . Apostolico se conspectui repraesentent."—*Compilatio* I, cc. 2, 9, 14, *de sententia excommunicationis,* V, 34; cc. 1, 7, 9, X, *de sententia excommunicationis,* V, 39; Jaffé, *Regesta Pontificum Romanorum* (ed. secundam correctam et auctam auspiciis Gulielmi Wattenbach curaverunt Kaltenbrunner ad annum 590, Ewald anno 590-882, Löwenfeld 882-1198, 2 vols. in 1, Lipsiae, 1885-1888), JL, nn. 12180, 14025, 13742. (Henceforth JK, JE, JL will signify the authors of this work.) Pope Clement III (1187-1191): ". . . pro absolutionis beneficio ad Apostolicam sedem sunt mittendi, . . ."—*Compilatio II,* c. 8, *de sententia excommunicationis,* V, 18; c. 19, X, *de sententia excommunicationis,* V, 39; JL, n. 16607; Pope Celestine III (1191-1198): ". . . quos etiam pro beneficio absolutionis habendo ad nos volumus cum litterarum tuarum insinuatione remitti"; ". . . excommunicationis sententiam donec ad Apostolicam sedem veniant, nequaquam evadunt."—*Compilatio II,* cc. 7, 13, *de sententia excommunicationis,* V, 18; cc. 18, 24, X, *de sententia excommunicationis,* V, 39; JL, nn. 17054, 17642, 17609; Pope Innocent III (1198-1216): ". . . mandamus, quatenus eos venire compellas ad sedem Apostolicam absolvendos. . . ."—*Compilatio III,* c. 11, *de sententia excommunicationis,* V, 21; c. 37, X, *de sententia excommunicationis,* V, 39; Potthast, *Regesta Pontificum Romanorum inde ab anno Post Christum Natum MCXCVIII ad Annum MCCCIV* (2 vols., Berolini, 1874-75), n. 2653. (Hereafter this work will be cited as Potthast.) Pope Gregory IX (1227-1241): ". . . non tamen taliter [aliter], quam per sedem Apostolicam vel eius legatum absolutionis potest beneficium obtinere, . . ."—c. 58, X, *de sententia excommunicationis,* V, 39; Potthast, n. 9689.

and thirteenth centuries used the term "reservation."[2] The term is also found in the *Extravagantes Communes.*[3]

In canon 15 of the II General Lateran Council (1139) the first general legislation of the Pope in reserving an excommunication to himself appears to be found. Prior to this law there existed about the ninth century the general custom of bishops sending penitents to Rome for absolution from certain sins, such as homicide and the malicious striking of a cleric, but this practice became so widespread that in the eleventh century superiors began to reserve to themselves absolution from certain sins and censures only.[4]

Pope Innocent II (1130-1143) placed upon those who had in-

---

[2] "Vel nisi absolutionem alii reservaverit, . . . ;"—Hostiensis, *Commentaria in Quinque Decretalium Libros,* tit. *de sententia excommunicationis,* c. *nuper* (V, 39, 29), v. *conditor canonis*—ed. Venetiis, apud Iuntas, 1581, V, fol. 113r, n. 16; ". . . hoc est verum nisi ubi lator canonis sibi sententiam specialiter reservavit. . . . Reservavit autem sibi dominus Papa absolutionem specialiter in casibus qui sequuntur."—Hostiensis, *Summa Aurea,* tit. *de sententia excommunicationis,* § *in supradictis casibus*—ed. Venetiis, 1570, fol. 499r, n. 12; ". . . Reservat autem Papa sibi absolutionem . . .—Sanctus Raymundus, *Summa,* lib. III, tit. 33, c. 3—ed. recognita et emendata, Veronae, 1744, p. 395; ". . . potest inferior absolvere si conditor canonis absolutionem sibi non reservavit. . . ."—Abbas Panormitanus, *Commentaria in Quinque Libros Decretalium,* tit. *de sententia excommunicationis* (V, 39, 29), v. *conditor canonis*—ed. Venetiis, 1588, p. 367, n. 5 and n. 6; cf. also *glossa* to c. 19, X, *de sententia excommunicationis,* V, 39, v. *publicati,* and *glossa* to c. 4, X, *de crimine falsi,* V, 20, v. *relaxari.*

[3] ". . . sicque de casibus, episcopis et superioribus, quos inferius adnotamus, ac sedi Apostolicae reservatis se nullatenus intromittant;"—c. 1, *de privilegis,* V, 7, in *Extrav. Comm.*: ". . . simili sententia . . . adstringimus; et reservantes nobis absolutionem eorum . . ."—c. 1, *de sententia excommunicationis,* V, 10, in *Extrav. Comm.* The laws cited are ascribed to Pope Boniface VIII (1294-1303).

[4] Thomassinus, *Vetus et Nova Ecclesiae Disciplina circa Beneficia et Beneficiarios* (Parisiis, 1688), Pars I, lib. 2, c. 13, n. 1. Thomassinus (*loc. cit.*) states that in early church legislation there existed no difference between cases reserved to the Pope and those reserved to the bishop; the bishops themselves would refer the decision concerning greater crimes to higher authority. Cf. also Dargin, *Reserved Cases According to the Code of Canon Law,* The Catholic University of America Canon Law Studies, n. 20 (Washington, D. C.: The Catholic University of America, 1924), p. 9. (Hereafter cited as *Reserved Cases.*)

curred an anathema for maliciously striking a cleric the obligation of presenting themselves before the Holy See, in order to obtain absolution. Only in danger of death did the reservation cease so that absolution could be granted by the bishop.[5]

Later Popes, however, relaxed the obligation of going to Rome for absolution from the above mentioned censure by excusing determined classes of persons from making the difficult journey. Pope Alexander III (1159-1181) considered as exempt from the obligation of recourse clerics under the age of puberty; monks and regulars; those clerics who, in exercising the office of *ostiariatus,* had struck another cleric without seriously injuring him; public officials; women and other persons who were not *sui iuris.*[6] In these exceptions no mention is made of later recourse, but those who for fear of enmity or for other just reasons could not present themselves before the Holy See, and had been absolved by their bishop, were excused from making a recourse only as long as the fear of enmity persisted or some other just reason perdured.[7] Concerning persons in high positions and those whose delicate condition would not permit them to make the journey without harm, the Roman Pontiff had to be consulted and his advice followed.[8]

Pope Clement III (1187-1191) added to the list of those who were exempted old men or others with physical defects. He placed upon the latter the obligation of recurring to Rome after they had regained their health.[9] In another place Pope Clement

[5] ". . . nullus episcoporum illum praesumat absolvere, nisi mortis urgente periculo, donec Apostolico conspectui presentetur et eius mandatum suscipiat." —c. 29, C. XVII, q. 4.

[6] *Compilatio* I, cc. 2-4, 7, *de sententia excommunicationis,* V, 34; cf. cc. 1-3, 6, *de sententia excommunicationis,* V, 39; (Jaffé, n. 8987) and JL, n. 13768.

[7] ". . . est illi sub iuramenti debito iniungendum, ut quam citius habuerit opportunitatem Romanum Pontificem adeundi, adeat mandatum Apostolicum suscepturus."—*Compilatio I,* c. 16, *de sententia excommunicationis,* V, 34; c. 11, X, *de sententia excommunicationis,* V, 39; JL, n. 13842.

[8] *Compilatio* I, c. 7, *de sententia excommunicationis,* V, 34; c. 6, X, *de sententia excommunicationis,* V, 39; JL, n. 13768.

[9] ". . . ut postquam sanitati fuerint restituti, ad Romanam ecclesiam vel eius legatum accedant, mandatum super talibus recepturi."—*Compilatio II,* c. 1, *de sententia excommunicationis,* V, 18; c. 13, X, *de sententia excomcunicationis,* V, 39; JL, n. 16623.

III, writing to the Bishop of Sigüenza, more clearly stated that dispensation was to be granted freely to persons of the feminine sex, boys and old men, and that no obligation of recourse was to be imposed, as was the case with those who had been absolved during illness.[10] The same Pontiff also granted an exemption to the poor and to those who were hindered by some inevitable and clear necessity, provided that the injury to the cleric was not enormous.[11] Comparing this exception with the statement made in Chapter One of the same title, one seems face to face with a contradiction.[12] This difficulty is solved, however, by a *glossa* in which it is explained that two classes of poor exist, namely, those who are poor but can nevertheless make the journey, and others whose poverty prevents them from doing so.[13]

A general summary of the impediments is given by Pope Celestine III (1191-1198), writing to the Bishop of Bruges, with the restatement that recourse to Rome had to be made after one's strength was regained and when an opportunity presented itself.[14]

Pope Innocent III (1198-1216) in the year 1202 conferred an explicit exemption upon nuns, and in the year 1206 specified under what circumstances a servant was not to be sent to Rome, namely, when damage would be suffered by the master as a result of the servant's departure, or when the servant was guilty of fraud or deceit, with the purpose of withdrawing himself from the obedience and allegiance due to his master.[15]

---

[10] *Compilatio II*, c. 6, *de sententia excommunicationis*, V, 18; compare c. 17, X, *de sententia excommunicationis*, V, 39; JL, n. 16596.

[11] *Compilatio II*, c. 3, *de sententia excommunicationis*, V, 18; compare c. 14 and 58, X, *de sententia excommunicationis*, V, 39; JL, n. 16637 and Potthast, n. 9689.

[12] ". . . alios autem sive pauperes, sive divites sedi Apostolicae vel eius delegato, ut beneficium absolutionis obtineat necesse est praesentari."—*Compilatio II*, c. 1, *de sententia excommunicationis*, V, 18; c. 13, X, *de sententia excommunicationis*, V, 39.

[13] *Glossa* to c. 13, X, *de sententia excommunicationis*, V, 39, v. *pauperes*.

[14] ". . . ut resumptis viribus et opportunitate concessa Romanam ecclesiam in persona propria debeant visitare."—*Compilatio III*, c. 15, *de sententia excommunicationis*, V, 18; c. 26, X, *de sententia excommunicationis*, V, 39—JL, n. 17612.

[15] *Compilatio III*, cc. 6 and 11, *de sententia excommunicationis*, V, 21; cc. 33 and 37, X, *de sententia excommunicationis*, V, 39; Potthast, nn. 1620, 2653.

Honorius III (1216-1227) about 1224 excused the Hospitallers of St. John of Jerusalem, except in a case of a serious inflicted injury.[16]

From the parallel reference to the decretals of Gregory IX (1227-1241), which were edited in the year 1234, it becomes clear that all these exemptions were incorporated into an authentic collection.

Pope Boniface VIII (1294-1303) added to the former legislation by determining that those who failed to make a recourse after the impediment ceased fell back into the same excommunication.[17]

Thus far the discussion has turned about the censure incurred for maliciously striking a cleric. Other censures were also reserved to the Pope. For example, Pope Alexander III (1159-1181) reserved to himself absolution from a suspension from office and benefice, if it was incurred by a priest for conferring a blessing upon those contracting second marriages.[18] Pope Clement III (1187-1191) placed a reservation on the excommunication incurred by those who were guilty of incendiarism and then were publicly denounced for it.[19]

The glossator of the Decretals of Gregory IX specifies that this decree refers to the burning of churches only, and that before any denunciation is made the *ipso iure* incurred excommunication is not reserved to the Pope. It is worthy of note to mention the fact that the glossator considered as the reason for the censure its being inflicted *in odium* of the culprit while the reason for the reservation was to deter others from the same crime.[20]

Pope Celestine III (1191-1198) added to these reserved censures two others: one, an excommunication incurred by clerics

---

[16] *Compilatio V*, c. 1, *de sententia excommunicationis*, V, 18; c. 50, X, *de sententia excommunicationis*, V, 39; Potthast, n. 7854.

[17] C. 22, *de sententia excommunicationis, suspensionis et interdicti*, V, II, in VI°.

[18] *Compilatio II*, c. un., *de secundis nuptiis*, IV, 15; c. 1, X, *de secundis nuptiis*, IV, 21—JL, n. 14180.

[19] *Compilatio II*, c. 8, *de sententia excommunicationis*, V, 18; c. 19, X, *de sententia excommunicationis*, V, 39—JL, n. 16607.

[20] Cf. *glossa* to c. 19, X, *de sententia excommunicationis*, V, 39, v. *publicati.*

who knowingly and willingly associated with those who were excommunicated by the Pope and received them in the celebration of the divine offices; another, an excommunication also, for the plundering of churches, which, however, became reserved only after a public denunciation was made.[21] Finally, Pope Innocent III (1198) reserved the absolution of those who had been excommunicated for knowingly retaining false documents ascribed to the Pope and for not destroying them or invalidating their effects within twenty days.[22]

ARTICLE II. RESERVATION OF CENSURES TO THE BISHOP

To understand the bishop's competence in relation to the reservation of censures it is necessary to remember that in the early centuries of the Church only bishops administered the sacrament of penance, and at first priests were allowed to absolve only when the bishop was absent or when he delegated the priest to do so.[23] When, however, more administrative matters arose and the number of faithful grew, the bishops gave faculties habitually and reserved only a certain number of cases or grievous crimes to their own judgment.[24] Both certain sins and certain censures, therefore, were reserved to the bishop's judgment. Most of the authors, until just before the Code, held the opinion that in an episcopal reservation of a crime with a censure attached both the sin and the censure were reserved separately.[25] The bishops in the ninth century of their own initiative sent penitents to Rome for absolution from the more grievous sins.[26]

---

[21] *Compilatio II*, cc. 7, 11, *de sententia excommunicationis*, V, 18; cc. 18, 22, X, *de sententia excommunicationis*, V, 39—JL, n. 17054, 17642.

[22] *Compilatio III*, c. 1, *de crimine falsi*, V, 11; c. 4, X, *de crimine falsi*, V, 20—Potthast, n. 202.

[23] Cf. Thomassinus, *Vetus et Nova Ecclesiae Disciplina circa Beneficia et Beneficiarios*, pars I, lib. 2, c. 14, n. 1.

[24] Thomassinus, *loc. cit.*

[25] Cf. *infra*, p. 36.

[26] Cf. Thomassinus, *ibidem*, c. 13, n. 1.

A. *Episcopal Jurisdiction in Relation to Censures in the* DECRETUM GRATIANI

In the *Decretum* of Gratian, which was issued about the year 1140, mention is found of the territorial limitation of the bishop to judge or excommunicate and also of the restriction of the bishop's jurisdiction to his own subjects.[27]

Rufinus (ca. 1190) asserts that everything which pertains especially to their own *parochiae* can be administered by the suffragans without the knowledge of the metropolitan, so that they are able to ordain clerics and excommunicate their own subjects.[28] This same jurisdiction was enjoyed by the metropolitan in regard to his own subjects.

If the suffragan bishop used his authority worthily, the metropolitan was not allowed in any way to condemn, absolve or even ordain clerics of the suffragan without consulting their bishop. However, if the suffragan absolved those that harmed or condemned the innocent, then the metropolitan was authorized to warn him to cease from such procedure, but was not empowered to nullify the act without consulting the suffragan himself. If after such an admonition the bishop continued to act wrongly, then the metropolitan had the power to rescind the action of the bishop.[29]

An additional limitation rested upon those who were inferior in authority, so that an inferior was unable to absolve a superior prelate.[30] Rufinus lists an exception to this principle. He states that one who is inferior in authority can nevertheless exercise power if he receives delegation from higher authority. He cites the example of a subdeacon who had received from the Pope a

---

[27] Pope Callistus I (217-222): "Nullus alterius terminos usurpet, nec alterius parochianum iudicare, vel ordinare, aut excommunicare praesumat, quia talis . . . excommunicatio . . . nec rata erit, nec vires ullas habebit, quoniam nullus alterius iudicis, nisi sui, sententia tenebitur, aut damnabitur" —JE, n. 86 (recorded as spurious): c. 1, C. IX, q. 2.

[28] *Summa Decretorum,* c. 1, C. IX, q. 3, v. *Quod Archiepiscopus*—ed. Singer (Paderborn, 1902), p. 300.

[29] Rufinus, *ibidem,* pp. 299, 300.

[30] C. 4, D. XXI.

delegation in some provinces and was thus authorized to condemn the guilty and absolve the innocent.[31] In this case the subdeacon was considered as acting in the name of the Holy See.

Appeals made exclusively to the metropolitan were the result of legislation which was later than the time of Gratian. In Gratian a person excommunicated by his bishop could not be received by other bishops, unless he had been received by his own bishop or had presented himself before a synod or council of bishops and had made satisfaction to the synod.[32] Neighboring bishops could be appealed to in a body and were competent as judges to decide whether the excommunication inflicted by a bishop was just or unjust.[33] But according to the glosses of a later date, the metropolitan alone was competent after an appeal to judge in causes of excommunication, and thereby presentation of one's self before a council of bishops as a means of redress became obsolete.[34] Also any appeal to neighboring bishops was considered as contrary to the then existing legislation.[35]

The power to excommunicate was considered as attached to the episcopal office.[36] In the *glossa ordinaria* to chapter four of the twenty-first distinction there is stated the rule which is frequently used by later authors, namely, he who can bind can also absolve and *vice versa*.[37] A priest could absolve from an excommunication inflicted by the bishop only when the penitent was in danger of death and the bishop happened to be absent.[38] This could be done even if the penitent was excommunicated *nominatim* by the bishop, but the reconciliation had to be private, because solemn reconciliation was reserved to the bishop alone.[39]

A priest also had the power to excommunicate according to the *glossa* to chapter eleven of Causa II, q. 1. As interpreted by

[31] Rufinus, *Summa Decretorum*, c. 4, D. XXI, v. *inferior*—Singer, p. 46.

[32] C. 2, C. XI, p. 3.

[33] C. 4, C. XI, q. 3.

[34] Cf. *glossa ord.*, to c. 2, C. XI, q. 3, v. *concilio*.

[35] Cf. *glossa ord.*, to c. 4, C. XI, q. 3, v. *interpellet*.

[36] Cf. *glossa ord.* to c. 17, C. XXIV, q. 3, v. *episcopale*.

[37] Cf. *glossa ord.* to c. 4, D. XXI, v. *inferior*.

[38] C. 5, C. XVI, q. 6; cf. also *glossa ord.* to *si episcopus*, of the same text.

[39] Rufinus, *Summa Decretorum*, c. 5, C. XXVI, q. 6, v. *Quod autem ab episcopo*—Singer, p. 428.

authors, this signified a priest who had some external jurisdiction, e.g., pastors. The archdeacon was likewise considered as having the same jurisdictional power.[40] If anyone had been excommunicated without a just cause, then he could appeal to the superior of the excommunicator, in order to free himself from the unjust excommunication.[41]

According to Rufinus, a person could be excommunicated in three ways, namely: (a) *propria sententia* for occult sins only; by the condemnation of his own conscience; (b) by an ecclesiastical sentence for manifest and criminal offenses; and (c) by an anathema, if out of contumacy the wrongdoer refused to make satisfaction for his crime.[42] The second excommunication involved a separation from the sacraments of the Church, and the author concluded that the excommunication inflicted either by the bishop or by a priest could be either of the last two types of excommunication.

B. *Episcopal Jurisdiction in Relation to Censures in the Decretals of Gregory IX*

At the close of the twelfth century and immediately preceding the Decretals of Pope Gregory IX (1234) the institute of episcopal reservation developed considerably. An intricate system of the reservation of and absolution from censures arose. Though as yet the term "reservation" was not used (even in the Decretals of Pope Gregory IX), still the episcopal censures were reserved as far as their effects were concerned. The authority of the metropolitan became noticeable in appeals from censures inflicted by the suffragans.

In one case the Bishop of Lisieux excommunicated his subjects, but the Archbishop of Rouen together with his suffragans refused to recognize the sentence of the bishop. Pope Innocent III in reply (1198) stated that an excommunication inflicted by any

---

[40] Cf. *glossa ord.* to c. 11, C. 2, q. 1; v. *excommunicet.*

[41] C. 11, C. 2, q. 1.

[42] *Summa Decretorum,* c. 2, C. 11, q. 3, v. *Si quis a proprio episcopo*—Singer, pp. 314 and 315.

one bishop should be observed by all, and that the excommunication was not suspended by an appeal, but that the penitent was to be sent to the bishop first. If the bishop refused absolution then the archbishop could absolve him, after receiving the required oath, to submit to the mandate of the excommunicator.[43]

In another case Pope Innocent III (1198-1216), writing to the Archbishop of Sens and his suffragans in the year 1203, clearly exemplified the jurisdictional limitation of the archbishop and the remaining suffragans in reference to a censure inflicted by a suffragan.[44] The case was the following: the Bishop of Auxerre had excommunicated his archpriest, who then appealed to the Archbishop of Sens. The archbishop advised the bishop to absolve the archpriest. After the bishop's refusal the archbishop granted absolution, but the bishop repudiated the absolution and referred the question to the Pope. The latter decided that, if an appeal was made after the sentence of excommunication had been promulgated, the metropolitan, before taking up the case, should absolve him with the oath, unless he preferred to defer the matter to the bishop. The archbishop was bound, however, to remit the penitent to the excommunicator if the excommunication had been incurred for an evident enormous crime. Therefore, the penitent could not receive absolution before the end of the trial, if he desired to prove the nullity of the sentence.

Both of these cases here listed were included in the third compilation, and twenty-four years later in the authentic collection of the Decretals of Pope Gregory IX.

There was a disputed doctrine among commentators relative to the validity of an absolution when it was granted by a metropolitan who disregarded the limitation imposed by the two above mentioned decisions.

Hugh of Pisa, known as Huggucio (d. 1210), Godfrey of Trani (d. 1245), and Henry of Susa (later Cardinal-Bishop of Ostia, hence "Hostiensis," d. 1271), opposed St. Raymond of

---

[43] *Compilatio III,* c. 2, *de officio iudicis ordinarii,* I, 20; c. 8, X, *de officio iudicis ordinarii,* I, 31; Potthast, n. 250.

[44] *Compilatio III,* c. 14, *de sententia excommunicationis,* V, 21; cf. also c. 40, X, *de sententia excommunicationis,* V, 39; Potthast, n. 1830.

Penyafort (b. about 1180; d. 1275), and maintained that, if the archbishop, *non ut iudex,* excommunicated a subject of the bishop, the sentence was not binding.[45] This lack of jurisdiction to excommunicate also implied the lack of jurisdiction to absolve.[46] The archbishop, however, had jurisdiction to absolve, but only in cases of appeal and in cases which were submitted to him during his visitation.

When there was question of an unjust excommunication it was immaterial whether or not the penitent appealed; the metropolitan could declare that the person had been unjustly bound without remitting the penitent to the suffragan for absolution.[47] If, on the contrary, the excommunication was just, then the metropolitan was obliged in every case to send the penitent to the excommunicator.[48] Other authors maintained that in cases both of just and of unjust excommunication the metropolitan was obliged to send the penitent to the bishop, and still other authors, as Godfrey of Trani, held that in neither case did the obligation involve a question of necessity, but rather one of courtesy.[49]

C. *Episcopal Jurisdiction in Relation to Censures in the* LIBER SEXTUS

The jurisdictional limitation of the archbishop in reference to excommunications inflicted on the subjects of his suffragans is clearly defined by Innocent IV (1243-1254). The Archdeacon of Poitiers, or the Abbot of the monastery of St. Cyprian, or perhaps some other prelate subject to the Bishop of Poitiers, had

[45] As cited by Henricus Boich, *Commentaria,* tit. *de officio iudicis ordinari,* c. *Pastoralis* (I, 31, 11)—ed. Venetiis: apud Haeredem Hieronymi Scoti, 1576, p. 138, n. 4.

[46] Henricus Boich *(loc. cit.)* states: "Quod dictum est de excommunicatione, idem intellige in absolutione, scilicet, quod si archiepiscopus absolvat de facto excommunicatos ab episcopo in casu non concesso a iure, quod non valet absolutio tamquam a non suo iudice facta."

[47] Cf. *glossa* to c. 40, X, *de sententia excommunicationis,* V, 39, v. *in Sardiciensi autem concilio.*

[48] Hostiensis, as cited by Henricus Boich, tit. *de sententia excommunicationis,* c. *Per tuas* (V, 39, 40)—*ibidem,* pp. 285-286, n. 4.

[49] Henricus Boich, *loc. cit.*

excommunicated his own subjects who in turn appealed directly to the metropolitan. This manner of proceeding was denounced by the Pope. The metropolitan, it was declared in this case, was judge neither of the one excommunicating nor of the one excommunicated, unless there existed a contrary custom.[50] If the metropolitan, disregarding this prohibition, nevertheless absolved the penitents, the absolution was invalid.[51]

The archbishop, moreover, was forbidden to constitute officials in a diocese of his suffragans for future causes to be decided by himself after an appeal, unless custom permitted the opposite.[52] The reason alleged was: before appeal the archbishop had no jurisdiction over the subjects of the bishop.[53] The glossator presented as a possibility the opinion that an excommunication inflicted by such an official of the archbishop upon the subjects of a suffragan was invalid, but he himself maintained the opposite.[54]

Further, if the sentence of excommunication was just, the superior judge (metropolitan), unless there was danger in delay, had to send the penitent to the excommunicator.[55] If the metropolitan was in doubt as to whether the sentence of excommunication was just or unjust, then the rule to be observed was the following:

> Quodsi dubitetur, utrum iusta sit vel iniusta: superior, nisi excommunicatori deferat, relaxare iuxta formam ecclesiae potest illam, quamquam honestius et convenientius agat si ei deferat in hoc casu. Ubi autem superiori competit de excommunicatione cognoscere: absolutio seu relaxatio, quam ipse fecerit, tenet, licet forsitan sit iniusta, quoniam, etsi contra ius litigatoris, non tamen contra ius constitutionis absolvit.[56]

---

[50] Cf. *casus* to c. 5, *de sententia excommunicationis, suspensioni et interdicti,* V, 11, in VI°.

[51] Cf. *glossa* to c. 5, *de sententia excommunicationis, suspensioni et interdicti,* V, 11, in VI°, *v. non relaxent.*

[52] C. 1, *de officio iudicis ordinarii,* I, 16, in VI°.

[53] Cf. Casus, to c. 1, *de officio iudicis ordinarii,* I, 16, in VI°.

[54] Cf. *glossa* to c. 1, *de officio iudicis ordinarii,* I, 16, in VI°, v. *non attentent.*

[55] C. 7, *de sententia excommunicationis, suspensionis et interdicti,* V, 11, in VI°; Potthast, n. 15454 (Innocent IV, 1254).

[56] C. 7, *de sententia excommunicationis, suspensionis et interdicti,* V, 11, in VI°.

ARTICLE III. RESERVED CENSURES

Further consideration is due to the jurisdictional power of the bishop in relation to the pope and other prelates, as interpreted by canonists of the twelfth and thirteenth centuries. There were especially two species of censures which were treated by the commentators and glossators of the decretals, the understanding of which throws light upon the institute of reservation as it then existed. They consist of censures incurred *ipso iure* and of censures inflicted *sententia iudicis.* These two types of censures had a different effect upon reservation. They will be treated successively in the immediately following two sections.

A. *Reservation of Censures Incurred* IPSO IURE

A censure could be inflicted *in modum canonis.* In order that the absolution from such a censure be reserved to the legislator *(lator canonis),* explicit mention of the reservation had to be made by the legislator.[57] If no explicit mention of the reservation was made, the censure was not reserved, and even those inferior to the one who enacted the censure could absolve their subjects from the censure.[58] Hostiensis enumerates thirty-three *ipso iure* contracted papal censures, and of these seven were reserved to the Pope.[59] These seven then were excluded from the jurisdiction of the bishop. Only when the penitent was in danger of death, or for some other equally serious canonical reason, did

[57] Cf. Hostiensis, *Summa Aurea,* tit. *de sententia excommunicationis,* § *quis possit ab hac sententia absolvere—ibidem,* fol. 499ᵛ, n. 12; Abbas Panormitanus, *Commentaria,* tit. *de sententia excommunicationis* (V, 39, 29), v. *conditor canonis—ibidem,* p. 367, n. 5; cf. also *glossa* to c. 29, X, *de sententia excommunicationis,* V, 39; *Compilatio III,* c. 3, *de sententia excommunicationis,* V, 21; Potthast, n. 700. During the vacancy of a diocese the cathedral chapter, or the one in whose hands the administration of the diocese was entrusted, had the power to absolve from all censures deriving *a iure* or *ab homine.* (Cf. c. unic., X, *de maioritate et obedientia,* I, 17.)

[58] Cf. Abbas Panormitanus, *loc. cit.*

[59] Hostiensis, *Summa Aurea,* tit. *de sententia excommunicationis,* § *quis possit excommunicare—ibidem,* fol. 492, n. 3 and fol. 499ʳ, n. 12.

the bishop have power to absolve.[60] Hostiensis gives as many as seventeen canonical reasons which may cause the papal reservation of the excommunication incurred for maliciously striking a cleric to cease.

Innocent III (1199) stated that not only the bishop but also priests, were able to absolve a penitent from the excommunication *(excommunicatio minor)* he had incurred by associating with an excommunicate who had contracted an *excommunicatio maior,* e.g., by eating or praying with the excommunicated party.[61] In accordance with the above mentioned statement, since the penitent was bound by a *sententia non iudicis sed iuris* inasmuch as no express mention of reservation had been made by the legislator, the bishop or *proprius sacerdos* could give absolution.[62] This declaration or statement made by Pope Innocent III, namely, for bishops and priests to absolve from an *excommunicatio minor* which was not reserved, was extended only later by the canonists to the *excommunicatio maior* and to other censures.[63]

If, on the other hand, the penitent had actively participated in the crime by aiding or favoring it, he incurred an *excommunicatio maior* and not an *excommunicatio minor,* and the absolution from the *excommunicatio maior* was then reserved to the legislator who in effect had precondemned the crime to which the reservation was attached. The bishop or *proprius sacerdos* could absolve when for a just reason recourse was difficult, but he previously had to put the penitent under oath to submit to the mandate of the excommunicator. This was allowed *"propter periculum animae."*[64] Another point to be mentioned in relation to an *excommunicatio maior* is that regularly no one except a bishop was to absolve solemnly from such a censure, regardless of the

---

[60] Hostiensis, *ibidem,* fol. 493r, n. 4.

[61] C. 29, X, *de sententia excommunicationis,* V, 39; *Compilatio III,* c. 3, *de sententia excommunicationis,* V, 21; Potthast, n. 700.

[62] Innocent III (1198-1216): ". . . quia tamen conditor canonis eius absolutionem sibi specialiter non retinuit, eo ipso concessisse videtur facultatem aliis relaxandi"—c. 29, X, *de sententia excommunicationis,* V, 39.

[63] Cf. Coronata, *Institutiones Iuris Canonici* (5 vols., Taurini: Marietti, 1928-1936), IV, 161, 162.

[64] Cf. *Casus* to c. 29, X, *de sententia excommunicationis,* V, 39.

fact whether or not it was reserved.[65] If, however, other prelates besides the bishop, such as abbots, archbishops, or archdeacons, did absolve, they were to do so without the solemn form.

Thus far the discussion has turned chiefly about the power of the bishop over his own subjects. If the person who participated in a crime which a bishop had condemned with a censure happened to be from another diocese, he then incurred a *sententia canonis* from which he could be absolved solely by the bishop who enacted the excommunication, and not by his own bishop. This was so because of the contempt of the *sententia canonis* of the extraneous bishop where the delict was committed. This opinion was followed by Hostiensis, Abbas Panormitanus (1386-1453) and Joannes Andreae (Giovanni D'Andrea, b. about 1275; d. 1348).[66]

B. *Reservation of Censures Inflicted* A IUDICE

The second species of excommunications treated by the authors and glossators consisted of *ferendae sententiae* excommunications. No one doubted that the bishop had the power to inflict a censure and reserve its absolution to himself. There were especially two principles which the decretalists and authors used in order to solve difficulties which arose concerning those who could inflict censures. The first principle was, "Excommunicatio spectat tantum ad officium episcopale, nam mucro episcopi dicitur."[67] The second principle was "Qui potest ligare, potest et solvere."[68]

---

[65] Cf. Abbas Panormitanus, *Commentaria,* tit. *de sententia excommunicationis* (V, 39, 29), v. *conditor canonis—ibidem,* p. 367, n. 6.

[66] As cited by Henricus Boich, *Commentaria,* tit. *de sententia excommunicationis,* c. *Nuper* (V, 39, 29)—*ibidem,* p. 275, n. 24; cf. also Hostiensis, *Lectura,* tit. *de sententia excommunicationis,* c. *Nuper* (V, 39, 29), v. *non iudicis—ibidem,* V, fol. 113 v., n. 14; Abbas Panormitanus, *Commentaria,* tit. *de sententia excommunicationis* (V, 39, 29), v. *tunc erit absolutio—ibidem,* p. 367, n. 9, 12; *glossa* to c. 20, X, *de foro competenti,* II, 2, v. *ratione delicti.*

[67] *Glossa* to c. 17, C. XXIV, q. 3; cf. Hostiensis, *Summa Aurea,* tit. *de sententia excommunicationis,* § *nedum autem ius—ibidem,* fol. 493^r, n. 5; Sanctus Raymundus, *Summa,* lib. III, tit. 33, c. 7—*ibidem,* p. 392.

[68] *Glossa* to c. 4, D. XXI; *Glossa* to c. 29, X, *de sententia excommunicationis,* V, 39, v. *tunc erit absolutio;* cf. Hostiensis, *Summa Aurea,* tit. *de sententia excommunicationis,* § *si vero sententia lata sit ab homine—ibidem,* fol. 500^r, n. 12.

From the second principle it was clear that the power of binding and the power of absolving were closely connected. Hostiensis, however, gives seven exceptions to this general rule, "qui potest ligare potest et solvere."[69] Among these exceptions are listed those sentences or penalties which may be inflicted by the ordinary or a delegate of the Holy See but the absolution of which is reserved to the Holy See, e.g., *excommunicatio maior* for certain crimes, as well as degradations, depositions, and excommunications inflicted by a delegate of the Pope after one year had elapsed from the time the censure was inflicted. This rule did not admit of any exceptions in cases in which a person had been excommunicated legitimately by a *sententia hominis* of one bishop and had asked for absolution from another bishop, even though the bishop asked was his own ordinary.[70]

An excommunication inflicted *ab homine* as a rule was reserved to the one who inflicted it. But the question as to who of those who were inferior to a bishop had the power to inflict excommunication was a matter of dispute among the authors. Hostiensis distinguishes three categories of opinions. Enumerated by him is first, the opinion of those who conceded the power only to the bishop; secondly, the opinion of others who extended that power to inferior prelates who presided over collegiate bodies, such as abbots whose incumbency had been confirmed and ratified, even though as yet they had not received their blessing; and finally, the opinion of those who asserted that every priest who had the care of souls had also the power to excommunicate.[71]

Basing their arguments upon the first principle mentioned above, some few authors contended that only bishops could ex-

---

[69] *Summa Aurea,* tit. *de sententia excommunicationis,* § *si vero sententia lata sit ab homine—ibidem,* fol. 500r, n. 12; cf. also *glossa ord.* to c. 4, D. XXI.

[70] Cf. *additio* to c. 29, X, *de sententia excommunicationis,* V, 39, c. *Nuper,* in *Commentaria,* Abbas Panormitanus—*ibidem,* p. 367r; cf. also Hostiensis, *Summa Aurea,* tit. *de sententia excommunicationis,* § *est et alia regula—ibidem,* fol. 501, v, n. 12.

[71] Cf. Hostiensis, *Summa Aurea,* tit. *de sententia excommunicationis,* § *nedum autem ius—ibidem,* fol. 493r, n. 5.

communicate persons.[72] Among these authors was Hugh of Pisa or Huggucio, as cited by St. Raymond of Penyafort.[73] As a consequence only the bishop as *lator sententiae* was considered to have power to absolve from the censure, if he had expressly reserved it. St. Raymond of Penyafort was of the view that abbots, archpriests, archdeacons and *Plebani* could inflict an *excommunicatio maior,* but without solemnity. Concerning priests of parochial churches, he stated that only by custom could they acquire jurisdiction to excommunicate. According to him the reason was: priests did not have the right over their subjects to judge them with ordinary jurisdiction, and hence could not inflict an *excommunicatio maior* unless custom permitted it.[74]

The same author held that, if the prelates inferior to the bishop inflicted an excommunication, granted that they had the jurisdiction, then the absolution granted by the bishop was valid.[75] The common opinion of authors held that a *simplex sacerdos* who did not have the care of souls, or of a parish, was unable to excommunicate because of the lack of the requisite jurisdiction. If, on the other hand, a priest had the care of souls or of a parish, he was unable to inflict solemn excommunication or *anathema,* but was able to inflict an *excommunicatio maior,* yet only when custom allowed it.[76]

Hostiensis, Joannes Andreae and Abbas Panormitanus specified that this power could not be extended to private persons even by custom, but only to prelates, such as archdeacons, archpriests and pastors. Abbas Panormitanus and Goffredus added that, if this power was not granted by custom to prelates of a rank inferior to that of a bishop, nevertheless it was granted by the common law (*iure communi*), as based upon the assertion in c.

---

[72] As cited by Hostiensis, *Summa Aurea,* tit. *de sententia excommunicationis,* § *nedum autem ius—ibidem,* fol. 493r, n. 4; Sanctus Raymundus, *Summa,* lib. III, tit. 33, c. 7—*ibidem,* p. 392.

[73] *Loc. cit.*

[74] *Loc. cit.*

[75] *Ibidem,* p. 395; cf. also Hostiensis, *Summa Aurea,* tit. *de sententia excommunicationis,* § *est et alia regula—ibidem,* fol. 501 v, n. 12.

[76] As cited by Henricus Boich, *Commentaria,* tit. *de officio iudicis ordinarii,* c. *Si Sacerdos* (I, 31, 2)—*ibidem,* pp. 134 and 135, nn. 1-4.

11, C. 2, q. 1. Some authors, among whom may be mentioned Joannes de Deo, professor of law at Bologna (1247-1253), held the contrary opinion, for, they asserted, an excommunication is to be inflicted only after the *cognitio causae*.[77] Hostiensis, however, stated that contrary custom and special delegation or concession could confer upon a priest the power to excommunicate even in cases which required judiciary procedure.[78]

The *ferendae sententiae* censures were to be considered as inflicted *ab homine*, but the extent of the *ab homine* inflicted censures was disputed. Some authors included all general and particular sentences inflicted for present contumacy, or for unrepented past offenses, e.g., under a phrase like the following, "we excommunicate those who have committed these offenses." Others were of the opinion that an *ab homine* derived censure was also that which was inflicted not only for past but also for future offenses upon a particular person or a group of persons, that is, as long as the legislator had no intention of enacting a general and abiding penal law which was to bind all subjects alike.[79]

---

[77] Henricus Boich, *ibidem*, n. 5.

[78] *Summa Aurea*, tit. *de sententia excommunicationis*, § *nedum autem ius*—*ibidem*, fol. 494v, n. 5.

[79] Cf. Hostiensis, *Summa Aurea*, annotatio c—*ibidem*, fol. 495r.

CHAPTER II

The Nature of Reservation

ARTICLE I. DEFINITION OF RESERVATION

In general, the term "to reserve" signifies the withholding or the limiting to one's self of a determined power with the purpose of excluding others from the use or further exercise of that power. Reservation designates the act by which the exercise of that certain power is limited or restricted to a determined superior. The power itself whose sphere of exercise becomes more limited in view of the reservation is called reserved. In canon law many things are reserved to determined superiors, e.g., the creation, re-establishment and suppression of cathedral and collegiate Chapters,[1] the establishing of dignitaries,[2] the conferring of dignities,[3] the absolution from sins,[4] the handling of causes of beatification,[5] the dispensation from certain vows,[6] the conferring of benefices,[7] the hearing of certain criminal cases,[8] the absolution from censures[9] and the penal suppression of an episcopal see.[10]

Reservation of censures essentially consists in the revocation or withdrawal of the absolving power over certain cases and the retention of the exclusive right of pronouncing judgment upon them. Such a reservation may be effected by those who have ordinary power to inflict penalties.[11] Superiors, then, if they

[1] Canon 329.

[2] Canon 394, § 2.

[3] Canon 396, § 1.

[4] Canons 893; 894.

[5] Canon 1999.

[6] Canons 1308, § 3; 1309.

[7] Canons 1431; 1434; 1435, § 1, § 2.

[8] Canons 1557, § 1; 2227, § 1.

[9] Canon 2245.

[10] Canon 2292.

[11] Canon 893, § 1. Qui ordinario iure possunt audiendi confessiones potestatem concedere aut ferre censuras, possunt quoque, excepto Vicario Capitulari et Vicario Generali sine mandato speciali, nonnullos casus ad suum avocare iudicium, inferioribus absolvendi potestatem limitantes.

have the right to transmit their jurisdiction to inferior judges, withhold the transferring of that jurisdiction by retaining the exclusive right to pronounce judgment. The immediate and primary purpose of reservation is to bring the more serious or difficult cases to the judgment of a higher court or a more competent judge.[12]

The imposition of a reservation by a superior affects directly the jurisdiction of the confessor who is the inferior judge, and only indirectly the penitent or culprit by way of consequence.[13] This becomes evident from a comparison with the civil and criminal procedure of every country which institutes courts of restricted and courts of general jurisdiction. In a similar manner the confessor, or any one endowed with jurisdiction in the external forum, may have a restricted or a general jurisdiction according to the amount of power assigned him by the superior who appoints him judge over crimes in their spiritual aspect.[14] Since the question of the primary and secondary purpose of reservation is

---

[12] Long before the Code the Council of Trent (Sess. XIV, *de poenitentia,* c. 7), on November 25, 1551, legislated: "Magnopere vero ad Christiani populi disciplinam pertinere sanctissimis patribus nostris visum est, ut atrociora quaedam et graviora crimina non a quibusvis, sed a summis dumtaxat sacerdotibus absolventur, unde merito pontifices maximi pro suprema potestate sibi in ecclesia universa tradita causas aliquas criminum graviores suo potuerunt peculiari judicio reservare. Neque dubitandum esset, quando omnia, quae a Deo sunt, ordinata sunt, quin hoc idem episcopis omnibus in sua cuique, dioecesi, in aedificationem tamen, non in destructionem liceat pro illis in subditos tradita supra reliquos inferiores sacerdotes auctoritate, *praesertim quoad illa, quibus excommunicationis censura annexa est.*" (Italics not in the original text.)

[13] Cf. Ayrinhac, *Legislation on the Sacraments in the New Code of Canon Law* (New York: Longmans, Green, 1928), p. 233. (Henceforth this work will be cited as *Legislation on the Sacraments.*) Coronata, *Institutiones Iuris Canonici,* IV, 160. Farrugia, *De Casuum Conscientiae Reservatione iuxta Codicem Iuris Canonici* (2. ed., Augustae Taurinorum-Romae: Marietti, 1922), p. 13, n. 5, a. (Hereafter cited as *De Casuum Conscientiae Reservatione.*) Marc-Gestermann-Raus, *Institutiones Morales Alphonsianae* (18. ed., 2 vols., Lugduni: Vitte, 1927), II, n. 1770. (Hereafter cited as *Institutiones.*)

[14] Cf. Woywod, *A Practical Commentary on the Code of Canon Law* (6. ed., 2 vols., New York: Wagner, 1941), I, n. 799. (Hereafter cited as *A Practical Commentary.*)

disputed, it will be treated more at length in the following two articles.

ARTICLE II. THE PRIMARY PURPOSE OF RESERVATION

The question as to whether or not there is contained a penal quality or the notion of penalty in the definition of reservation is definitely solved by the Code. The Code in defining reservation excluded the notion of penalty.[15]

Before the Code the question was disputed. Many authors were of the opinion that reservation, considered in its own intrinsic purpose, in its *finis operis* as opposed to the *finis operantis*, was penal.[16] Ojetti[17] who adhered to the opposite opinion to-

---

[15] Canon 893, § 1. Cf. Ayrinhac, *Legislation on the Sacraments*, p. 234; Cappello, *De Censuris iuxta Codicem Iuris Canonici* (3. ed., Taurinorum Augustae: Marietti, 1933), n. 72. (Hereafter cited as *De Censuris.*) Coronata, *loc. cit.*; Darmanin, "De Reservatione Peccatorum Iure Codicis Piano-Benedictini,"—*Angelicum* (*Unio Thomistica*, Romae, 1924-; ab anno 1295; *Angelicum*), V (1928), 213-223. (Hereafter cited as *De Reservatione Peccatorum.*) The reader is cautioned to remember that Darmanin *ex professo* treats of the reservations of sins and not censures, but those arguments which may also be applied to the reservation of censures are taken into consideration in the following instances where his article is cited. These arguments confirm the non penal character not only of the reservation of sins but also of the reservation of censures. Dargin, *Reserved Cases*, p. 16; Marc-Gestermann-Raus, *Institutiones*, II, nn. 1766, 1770; Swoboda, *Ignorance in Relation to the Imputability of Delicts*, The Catholic University of America Canon Law Studies, n. 143 (Washington, D. C.: The Catholic University of America Press, 1941), p. 229; Sipos, *Enchiridion Iuris Canonici ad Usum Scholarum et Privatorum* (Pécs: ex Typographia "Haladás, R. T.," 1926), p. 916. (Hereafter cited as *Enchiridion.*)

[16] Gury-Ballerini, *Compendium Theologiae Moralis* (3. ed., 2 vols., Romae, 1874-1875), II, 472-476; Ballerini-Palmieri, *Opus Theologicum Morale* (7 vols., Prati, 1889-1893), n. 481; Lehmukuhl, *Theologia Moralis* (6. ed., 2 vols., Friburgi Brisgoviae: Herder, 1890), II, 294-295; Lega (*Praelectiones in Textum Iuris Canonici, De Iudiciis Ecclesiasticis* [4 vols., Romae, 1896-1901], IV, 124) maintained that reservations of *latae sententiae* inflicted censures took on the nature of a penalty and that, to safeguard the efficacy of this penalty, the Constitution "*Apostolicae Sedis*" decreed an excommunication upon all who presumed to absolve from censures reserved *speciali modo* to the Holy See without special faculties. Cf. also *Il Monitore Ecclesiastico* (Romae, 1876-), XXVIII (1915), 378; Hollweck, *Die kirchlichen Strafgesetze* (Mainz, 1899), p. 107, note 1.

[17] *Synopsis Rerum Moralium et Iuris Pontificii* (Romae, 1899), "Reservatio casuum," p. 453.

gether with other authors,[18] admitted that the assertion of those authors who vouched for the penal quality of reservation did not lack at least extrinsic probability and that as a consequence in practice a confessor was able to absolve a penitent, if he was ignorant of the reservation of the sin or the censure.

Even after the Code there are found some authors who defend the penal nature of reservations.[19] Farrugia asserts that the reservation of the censure as well as the censure itself is inflicted as a punishment, and, he states, since the opinion is at least probable, the opinion can be followed in practice. There exists, he says, a *dubium iuris,* and according to canon 209 the Church supplies jurisdiction in a positive and probable doubt of law.[20] Chelodi states that the reservation of the sin of false accusation of solicitation is penal according to the common opinion.[21]

A few authors are inclined to reject as improbable the opinion

---

[18] Alphonsus, *Theologia Moralis* (ed. novissima, 10 vols. in 5, Mechliniae, 1852), lib. VI, nn. 580, 581; Bucceroni, *Institutiones Theologiae Moralis secundum Doctrinam S. Thomae et S. Alphonsi* (3. ed., 2 vols., Romae, 1898), II, n. 796; (hereafter cited as *Institutiones Theologiae Moralis*); D'Annibale, *Summula Theologiae Moralis* (5. ed., 3 vols., Romae, 1908), I, 343; Lugo, *Disputationes Scholasticae et Morales* (ed. nova, 8 vols., Pariis, 1868-1869), *De Sacramento Poenitentiae,* disp. 20, sec. 1, n. 11; Sanchez, *Disputationum de Sancto Matrimonio Tomi Tres* (3 vols., Lugduni: Arisson, 1739), lib. IX, disp. 32, n. 18; Ojetti, however, excepted from this general rule the reservation expressly imposed as a penalty for the crime of false denunciation in the confessional—*loc. cit.*

[19] The penal nature of reservations after the Code was defended by Farrugia (*De Casuum Conscientiae Reservatione,* pp. 13, 29, 30) and Arregui (*Summarium Theologiae Moralis ad Recentem Codicem Iuris Canonici Accomodatum* [10. ed., Bilbao: El Mensajero del Corazon de Jesus Apartado 73, 1927], p. 607, note 1, and p. 886).

[20] *Ibid.,* p. 30; cf. *infra,* p. ??, where the force of Farrugia's arguments is considered.

[21] Chelodi, speaking of the crime of false accusation of solicitation, says: ". . . Hucusque *peccatum* erat ratione sui specialissimo modo reservatum; nunc quoque est reservatum (can. 894): quomodo disputant auctores, sed, uti videtur, otiose, quia a Pontifice tandem pendet utrum et cui velit facultatem absolvendi delegare. Reservatio, ex communi sententia, est poenalis."—*Ius Poenale et Ordo Procedendi in Iudiciis Criminalibus iuxta Codicem Iuris Canonici* (Tridenti, 1925 [1920?]), n. 88. (Hereafter cited as *Ius Poenale.*)

upholding the penal nature of reservation. Coronata states definitely that the opinion unholding the penal nature of reservation has at least extrinsic probability, but is not based on a solid foundation.[22] Vermeersch-Creusen do not as yet dare to reject the extrinsic probability of the more lenient view—that ignorance excuses the penitent from the reservation—but do reject the intrinsic probability of that view.[23] Ayrinhac simply denies the intrinsic probability of the opinion which upholds the penal nature of reservation, without mentioning at all the extrinsic probability of that opinion.[24]

Noldin-Schmitt assert that there is no trace of a penal notion attached to reservation in the Code, but maintain that the added purpose of reservation of sins is medicinal, namely, to deter the faithful from sins inasmuch as they would realize the difficulty of obtaining absolution.[25] Noldin-Schmitt state that ignorance of the reservation of sins reserved *ratione sui* does not excuse one from the reservation because reservation is not penal, and that ignorance of the *poenae* in reference to sins reserved *ratione censurae* is governed by canon 2229. This is perfectly true, but there still remains the question of penal or non-penal nature of the reservation itself of censures (i.e., sins reserved *ratione censurae*). Surely canon 2229 does not answer this question, since canon 2229 deals with the ignorance of the *poenae*. The reservation itself of the censure or *poenae* is not a penalty and can not be governed by the rules of canon 2229. This Noldin-Schönegger admit.[26] The non-penal nature of the reservation both of sins and of censures is essential to the concept of reservation.

---

[22] *Ibid.*, 160, note 1.

[23] *Epitome Iuris Canonici cum Commentariis ad Scholas et ad Usum Privatum* (3. ed., 3 vols., Mechlinae-Romae: Dessain, 1927-1928), II, n. 174. (Hereafter cited as *Epitome.*)

[24] *Ibid.*, p. 235.

[25] ". . . eo autem quod postulatur, ne reservatio diutius in vigore manet, quam necesse sit ad publicum aliquod vitium exstirpandum et collapsam christianam disciplinam restaurandam innuitur finis *medicinalis,* qui etiam ex eo apparet, quod Ordinarius curare debet, ut reservationes dioecesanae ad subditorum notitiam deducantur."—Noldin-Schmitt, *Summa Theologiae Moralis iuxta Codicem Iuris Canonici* (23. ed., 3 vols., Oeniponte-Rauch: Pustet, 1935), III, n. 358. (Hereafter cited as *Summa Theologiae Moralis.*)

[26] *De Censuris* (29. ed., Oeniponte: Rauch, 1935), n. 24. Cf. also Noldin-Schmitt, *Summa Theologiae Moralis,* n. 363.

Marc-Gestermann invert the order of the purposes of reservation as established by Noldin-Schmitt and assert that the purpose of reservation is especially medicinal.[27] To call the purpose of reservation "medicinal" implies no more than a veering away from the concept of vindicative punishment. The very purpose of a punishment or of a penalty may equally well be of a medicinal character.

After the Code a reservation, whether of a sin or of a censure, must be considered an administrative limitation of the jurisdiction of inferior confessors, and the opposite view has no foundation and today can scarcely be said to have even extrinsic probability.[28] This assertion is in perfect harmony with the declaration of the Code Commission according to which a *peregrinus* is bound by the reservations of the place in which he is.[29] It appears evident that, if the *peregrinus* is bound by the reservation of sins, then his ignorance which is easily presumed in one not of the diocese does not exempt him. Yet this ignorance would surely exempt him, if the reservation were penal in character.

One can consider the purpose or end of reservation itself without considering the purpose intended by the legislator, and one must logically conclude that the imposition of a reservation acts neither as a punishment for the priest whose jurisdiction is limited nor as a punishment for the penitent. Reservation does not act as a punishment for the priest, for there is no transgression of any law on the part of the priest, inasmuch as the restriction of jurisdiction affects every single priest and all priests alike without distinction. Reservation does not act as a punishment for the penitent, for the reservation of the sin or of the censure does not primarily affect the penitent or the sinner, but rather attends to the sin or censure considered in itself, or the gravity of the sinful act.[30]

---

[27] *Institutiones*, II, 1766. Cf. also *infra*, footnote n. 34.

[28] Dargin, *Reserved Cases*, p. 16; Swoboda, *Ignorance in Relation to the Imputability of Delicts*, p. 229.

[29] *AAS*, XII (1920), 575. Cf. also Vermeersch, "Annotationes"—*Periodica* (*Periodica de Re Canonica et Morali utili Praesertim Religiosis et Missionariis, Bruges*, 1905—ab anno 1927: *Periodica de Re Canonica, Morali, Liturgica*), X (1922), 255, 256.

[30] Cf. Darmanin, "De reservatione peccatorum,"—*Angelicum*, V (1928), 213-215.

One cannot deny that there is some inconvenience *(gravamen)* imposed upon the penitent who cannot be absolved by any confessor, but must seek either the superior to whom the sin or censure is reserved or a confessor who has special faculties. But this inconvenience is not intended to act as a punishment. In reality, rarely is the reservation so limited to only one superior that one could consider it as a punishment. Moreover, no one can say that, if a person is to present his case to a competent judge, the inconvenience caused by the seeking of even the one competent judge is a punishment.[31] The common good of society requires that certain more grievous sins and abuses be brought to the attention of the higher superiors who are better fit to judge the case and apply remedies. The Code itself determines reservation as a disciplinary measure for the right administration of the faithful.[32]

Since the legislator excludes from the definition of reservation the notion of penalty and explicitly ordains the reservation to serve as a disciplinary measure, the primary purpose of reservation undoubtedly is not penal, i.e., to serve as a punishment for the culprit. The censure itself fulfills this end. The primary purpose of reservations is to bring more serious crimes to the judgment of more prudent superiors by limiting the jurisdiction of inferior confessors. Reservation primarily affects the jurisdiction of the confessor, and only secondarily the penitent. The primary purpose, therefore, is disciplinary, which provides for the maintaining of ecclesiastical discipline and the correcting of the morals of the faithful. The object with which the reservation is primarily concerned is the very crime itself.[33]

---

[31] Darmanin, *ibid.*, pp. 216-218.

[32] Canon 897.—Casus reservandi sint pauci omnino, tres scilicet, vel ad summum, quattuor ex gravioribus tantum et etrocioribus criminibus externis specifice determinatis; ipsa vero reservatio ne ultra in vigore maneat, quam necesse sit ad publicum aliquod inclitum vitium exstirpandum et collapsam forte christianam disciplinam instaurandam. This canon deals with the reservation of sins only, while canon 2246, § 1, which treats of the reservation of censures reads as follows: "Ne reservetur censura, nisi attenta peculiari gravitate delictorum et necessitate aptius providendi disciplinae ecclesiasticae et medendi conscientiis fidelium."

[33] Canon 897.—Casus reservandi sint pauci . . . *ex gravioribus tantum et atrocioribus criminibus externis*. . . .

ARTICLE III. IS THERE A SECONDARY PURPOSE OF RESERVATION?

The secondary purpose of reservation which is under discussion is not to be confused with the purpose which is intended by the superior who determines the reservation. As in the preceding article, so here there is question of the purpose of reservation considered in itself and not in connection with the intention of the superior.

Marc-Gestermann-Raus maintain that the purpose of reservation is disciplinary and medicinal, and especially medicinal, which purpose is adduced from the words of the Council of Trent (Sess. XIV, *de poenitentia*, c. 7).[34] Noldin-Schmitt consider the disciplinary purpose and the medicinal purpose as equal. The latter purpose is evident from the fact that the Ordinary should see to it that the knowledge of diocesan reservations be brought to the subjects.[35] Ayrinhac[36] considers as a second purpose of reservation the correction or the punishment of the individual sinner. Cappello,[37] Coronata,[38] Dargin,[39] Vermeersch-Creusen[40] and Swoboda[41] definitely exclude the penal character of reserva-

---

Canon 2246, § 1. Ne reservetur censura, *nisi attenta peculiari gravitate delictorum*. . . . (Italics not in original text.)

Cf. Coronata, *Institutiones Iuris Canonici*, IV, 160; Darmanin, *ibid.*, pp. 213-215.

[34] *Institutiones*, II, n. 1766. Marc-Gestermann-Raus present four purposes of reservation. They assert: "Finis reservationis est: 1° *ut disciplinae nervus* servetur, quatenus convenit atrociora delicta puniri; 2° ut subditi efficacius *absterreantur* a delictis, quorum remissionem viderint difficiliorem; 3° ut in istiusmodi peccata prolapsi accipiant *congruas poenitentias*, admonitiones et remedia, quae efficacius a Superioribus dantur; 4° ut *ordo turbatus* securius vindicetur. Finis igitur reservationis est *disciplinaris;* praecipue tamen est *medicinalis*."

[35] *Summa Theologiae Moralis*, III, n. 358. Here Noldin-Schmitt refer to sins reserved *ratione sui*.

[36] *Legislation on the Sacraments*, pp. 233, 234. Here he states: "Reservation may have also, although only mediately and objectively speaking secondarily a corrective and punitive effect on the individual sinner. . . ."

[37] *De Censuris*, n. 72.

[38] *Institutiones Iuris Canonici*, IV, 160.

[39] *Reserved Cases*, p. 16.

[40] *Epitome*, II, 174.

[41] *Ignorance in Relation to the Imputability of Delicts*, p. 229.

tions, but they do not enter into the consideration of the secondary or subordinate purpose of reservations, and do not consider whether the secondary purpose of reservations themselves could possibly be medicinal, namely the correction of the penitent.

When one is cognizant of the fact that reservation is determined for the common good of society and not for the private good of the individual, it appears clear that the secondary end of reservation is of itself neither medicinal nor punitive; for, there is no connection between the obligation of seeking a determined confessor and the duty of emendation, since the more difficult the obtaining of absolution becomes, the people are less inclined to approach the confessional.[42] Only in certain circumstances and for particular instances, and hence only incidentally can the secondary purpose of reservation be considered as medicinal. Therefore it is evident that, since a reservation is medicinal only by way of incidental occurrence, the reservation considered in its nature or considered in itself cannot be said to be medicinal even secondarily, and much less can a medicinal purpose be termed an *alter finis* of reservation.[43]

ARTICLE IV. THE PURPOSE INTENDED BY THE SUPERIOR FOR THE RESERVATION

Thus far the primary purpose or end of reservation considered in itself has been determined. A few statements remain to be made in reference to the purpose which is intended (or affixed to the reservation) by the superior who imposes the reservation upon a sin or a censure. The question, then, to be answered is concerned with the purpose intended by the superior, or the *finis operantis*. No one can deny that the legislator, in determining a reservation, is able to attach either a penal or a medicinal purpose to his act of reservation.[44]

[42] Darmanin, *De Reservatione Peccatorum,—Angelicum,* V (1928), 220, 221.

[43] Cf. Darmanin, *art. cit.,* p. 222.

[44] Cf. Darmanin, "*De Reservatione Peccatorum,*"—*Angelicum,* V (1928), 224; Dargin, *Reserved Cases,* p. 11; Farrugia, *De Casuum Conscientiae Reservatione,* p. 12. Benedict XIV in the year 1741 expressly imposed as a penalty a reservation of the sin *ratione sui* for the crime of false denunciation of solicitation in the confessional; cf. *Bullarium Benedicti XIV* (ed. nova, 13 vols., Mechliniae, 1826-1827), I, p. 104, § 3.

Most of the authors who deal with the purpose of reservation do not advert to this precise distinction. This fact probably explains why some of them consider the medicinal purpose as the *finis operis* of a reservation. The following authors do not advert to the distinction: Ayrinhac, Cappello, Coronata, Marc-Gestermann-Raus, Noldin, Swoboda and Vermeersch-Creusen. Ayrinhac, Marc-Gestermann-Raus and Noldin, instead of placing the medicinal or punitive end of reservation under the *finis operantis* of a reservation, place the medicinal (as Marc-Gestermann and Noldin) or punitive (as Ayrinhac) end under the *finis operis* of a reservation.

The question which now remains to be solved is whether the intention of the legislator was manifested in determining the purpose of reservation (the *finis operantis* of a reservation).

Farrugia proposes the following facts and conclusions. In reference to the reservation of censures which are reserved to the Holy See or to the bishop by the legislation of the common law, the mind of the Church was not made manifest until the Instruction of the Holy Office on the 13th of July, 1916,[45] and until the appearance of that Instruction the probable opinion favored the imposition of reservation as a medicinal punishment, since every reservation not only *de facto* but also *ex intentione Ecclesiae* acts as a punishment for sinners and as a deterrent to more serious delinquencies.[46] Farrugia concludes that in the present legislation it is safe to hold the proposed probable view, since, as he maintains, the Church manifested its intention when in the above mentioned Instruction and in canon 897 it declared that any reservation whatsoever determined by an Ordinary is not incurred by those who are ignorant of the reservation. It must be noted, however, that such a statement is found neither in the Instruction nor in canon 897; to the contrary, only an intended medicinal purpose, not punitive, can be deduced from the two mentioned sources, and therefore Farrugia's conclusion cannot be accepted. The canon which deals with the purpose of the reservation of censures must accordingly receive some

[45] *Acta Apostolicae Sedis, Commentarium Officiale,* VIII (1916), 313-315. Hereafter cited as *AAS.*

[46] *De Casuum Conscientiae Reservatione,* p. 13.

consideration, and thereupon the Instruction of 1916 may be examined in greater detail.

Canon 2246 states that a censure should not be reserved unless the peculiar gravity of the offenses and the necessity of maintaining ecclesiastical discipline and the correcting of the morals of the faithful demand the reservation. Three factors must be considered before a reservation is imposed, namely, the gravity of the offense, the necessity of maintaining ecclesiastical discipline and the necessity of correcting the morals of the faithful. The consideration of any penal factor is omitted. Therefore, it can rightly be concluded that the Code intends the reservation of censures to be used as a disciplinary and a medicinal means, and excludes from the *finis operantis* any penal measure. This conclusion is confirmed when one considers similar legislation in reference to the reservation of sins.[47]

The Instruction of the Holy Office issued in the year 1916 does mention the reservation of censures, but does not even hint that the purpose intended is penal. The words of the Instruction are the following:

> Cauti insuper omnino sint et quam maxime parci quod ad poenales sanctiones, excommunicationes praesertim, quibus forte suas reservationes communiri velint; nam, ut sapienter admonet Sacrosancta Tridentina Synodus (Sess. 25, *de ref.*, c. 3): "Quamvis excommunicationis gladius nervus sit ecclesiasticae disciplinae et ad continendos in officio populos valde salutaris; sobrie tamen magnaque circumspectione exercendus est, cum experientia doceat, si temere aut levibus ex rebus incutiatur, magis contemni quam formidari et perniciem potius parere quam salutem."[48]

Therefore it rightly can be concluded that before the Code in the Instruction of the Holy Office (1916) and after the Code

---

[47] Canon 897.—Casus reservandi sint pauci omnino, tres scilicet, vel, ad summum, quatuor ex gravioribus tantum et atrocioribus criminibus externis specifice determinatis; ipsa vero reservatio ne ultra in vigore maneat, quam necesse sit ad publicum aliquod inolitum vitium exstirpandum et collapsam forte christianam disciplinam instaurandam.

[48] *AAS*, VIII (1916), 314, n. 5.

the expressed intention of the Church for determining reservations of censures does not show any traces of punishment.

ARTICLE V. COMPARISON OF THE KINDS OF RESERVATIONS

The reservation of sins differs from the reservation of censures, as is stated in the Code.[49] Canon 894 reserves the sin of falsely accusing a priest of solicitation and in the fifth book the same sin is reserved with a censure.[50] This demonstrates that the same delict is punished by different reservations; there would be no need of the repetition if the reservation of sins did not differ from the reservation of censures. Each kind of reservation is governed by different canons,[51] and the violations of the prescripts of each are punished by different penalties.[52]

The radical power to absolve from sin is received in ordination, but in addition jurisdiction is required for the exercise of this power. The jurisdiction granted by the Ordinary may also be limited by him, the power to absolve from censures comes in general from the superior who inflicted or constituted them.[53]

---

[49] Canon 893, § 3. Quod attinet ad reservationem censurarum, servetur praescriptum can. 2246, 2247.

Cf. also Ayrinhac, *Legislation on the Sacraments*, p. 238; Cappello, *De Censuris*, n. 66; Coronata, *Institutiones Iuris Canonici*, IV, 160; De Meester *Juris Canonici et Juris Canonico-Civilis Compendium* (nova ed., 3 vols. in 4, Brugis: Desclée, 1921-1928), III, n. 1736. Hereafter cited as *Compendium*.)

[50] Canon 2263.

[51] The reservation of sins is governed by canons 893-900, while that of censures by canons 2245-2254. Few authors attempted to apply the rules of the reservation of sins to the reservation of censures. Cf., e.g., Mothon, *Institutions Canoniques a L'usage des Curies Episcopales, du Clerge Paroissial, et des Familles Religieuses* (2 vols., Societé Saint-Augustin: Desclée, 1924), II, p. 163, note 7.

[52] Canon 2338 contains the punishment for violation of the reservation of censures and canon 2366 for violation of the reservation of sins.

[53] Ayrinhac, *Legislation on the Sacraments*, pp. 238-239; Coronata, *op. cit.*, IV, 160; Sole, *Praelectiones in Lib. V Codicis Iuris Canonici—De Delictis et Poenis* (Romae: Pustet, 1920), n. 170. (Hereafter cited as *De Delictis et Poenis.*) Absolution from a reserved sin pertains to the internal forum, while absolution from a reserved censure pertains to the external forum although absolution may be granted in the internal forum when the good of souls demands it.—Ayrinhac, *loc. cit.;* Sole, *loc. cit.*

One sin is reserved to the Holy See in itself, *ratione sui,* and this implies that sins are also reserved indirectly or *ratione alterius.*[54] A sin can be reserved in itself, directly or immediately, as is done according to the rules of canons 895-898.

The reservation of the sin *ratione sui* affects not only the licitness but also the validity of the absolution.[55]

Further, a sin can be reserved indirectly or mediately, not in itself but by reason of something else which is attached to the sin and because of which secondarily or accessorily the reservation affects the sin. Mention of this latter kind of reservation of the sin occurs in canon 2246, § 3.[56] This sin is said to be reserved *ratione censurae.* The Code itself uses this terminology.[57] Finally, there is the reservation which affects only the censure and not the sin.[58] In this case the censure alone is reserved, and

---

[54] Canon 894; cf. also Ayrinhac, *ibid.,* pp. 236-237; Darmanin, *art. cit.,* p. 63; Marc-Gestermann-Raus, *Institutiones,* II, n. 1766; Blat, *Commentarium Textus Codicis Iuris Canonici* (6 vols., Rome, 1920-1927), lib. III, *De Rebus,* Pars I (1924), p. 259 (hereafter cited as *De Rebus*). Dargin, *ibid.,* pp. 4, 5; Farrugia, *De Casuum Conscientiae Reservatione,* pp. 13-14. Farrugia, however, adds a third distinction, namely, *cum censura,* which occurs when a sin is reserved *ratione sui* and an excommunication reserved or non-reserved is attached. But, in effect, these combinations are reducible to either the one or the other of the two mentioned.

[55] Before the Code the Council of Trent (Sess. XIV, *de poenitentia,* can. 11) had decreed: "Si quis dixerit, episcopos non habere just reservandi sibi casus, nisi quoad externam politiam, atque ideo casuum reservationem non prohibere, quominus sacerdos a reservatis vere absolvat: anathema sit." Cf. Ayrinhac, *ibid.,* p. 237.

[56] Reservatio censurae impedientis receptionem Sacramentorum importat reservationem peccati cui censura adnexa est; verum si quis a censura excusatur vel ab eadem fuit absolutus, reservatio peccati penitus cessat.

Cf. also canon 2275, 2°, which prohibits those who are personally interdicted the use of the Sacraments, and canon 2250, which prohibits the absolution from sins, unless the penitent has first received absolution from the censure which impedes the reception of sacraments. Cf. also Ayrinhac, *loc. cit.;* Cappello, *De Censuris,* n. 70; Coronata, *op. cit.,* IV, 161; Darmanin, *ibid.,* p. 66; Farrugia, *loc. cit.;* Marc-Gestermann, *loc. cit.*

[57] Canon 898.—Prorsus ab iis peccatis sibi reservandis omnes abstineant quae iam sint Sedi Apostolicae etiam *ratione censurae* reservata. . . . (Italics not in original.)

[58] Canon 2250, § 1. Si agatur de censura quae non impedit Sacramentorum receptionem, censuratus, rite dispositus et a contumacia recedens, potest absolvi a peccatis, firma censura.

not the sin which is the cause of the censure. The Code defines reservation by reason of censure as a limitation of jurisdiction[59] which clearly pertains to the validity of absolution from the sin and the censure when there is question of a censure which impedes the reception of sacraments. The opinion, therefore, which asserts that only the jurisdiction in reference to the censure is withheld so that all confessors would still possess jurisdiction in reference to the sin when it is reserved *ratione censurae* can not be upheld.[60]

The local Ordinary can establish or enact the reservation of a sin *ratione sui* only after discussing the matter in a diocesan synod, or outside the synod with the Cathedral Chapter and some of the more prudent and experienced priests exercising the care of souls. Four cases at the most can be reserved.[61] Reservation of censures, on the other hand, is not limited by these restrictions. Reservation of a sin *ratione sui* in exempt religious organizations is restricted to the superior general, and in monastic orders, to the abbot of an autonomous monastery, with their respective councils;[62] reservation of censures can be made by all Ordinaries (i.e., provincials of exempt religious orders and congregations).[63]

The cases in which the reservation of the sin reserved *ratione sui* ceases are enumerated in canon 900, and do not apply to the cessation of the reservation of censures, which is regulated by the canons of the fifth book of the Code.[64] Greater facility is granted for the absolution of sin reserved *ratione sui* than for that of reserved censures which are incurred only after full knowledge and contumacy.[65] One absolved by a confessor not

---

[59] Canon 893, § 1. Cf. also Ayrinhac, *loc. cit.*

[60] Farrugia (*loc. cit.*) states: "Peccatum est reservatum *ratione censurae*, quando reservatio cadit in censuram peccato adnexam, et *mediate* tantum in peccatum. In tali casu iurisdictio non aufertur in peccatum, sed in solam censuram ita ut communis confessarius possit quidem valide absolvere *a peccato*, non vero *a censura* si Superior contrarium non expresserit. . . ." This assertion of Farrugia can only refer to sins reserved by reason of a censure which does not impede the reception of sacraments.

[61] Canons 895; 897.

[62] Canon 896.

[63] Cf. canons 2220; 2245, § 2.

[64] Canons 2245-2254.

[65] Compare canons 899; 900 with canons 2252; 2254.

possessing faculties from a sin reserved *ratione sui* in cases of necessity is not obliged to make a recourse, while after absolution from reserved censures in certain cases of necessity recourse is prescribed.[66] Reservation of a sin alone and the reservation of a censure do not bind the penitent outside of the superior's territory,[67] except, of course, *ab homine* inflicted censure.[68]

ARTICLE VI. A RESERVED CASE

A. *Historical Notes*

The Council of Trent (1545-1563) treated the reservation of sins and the reservation of censures in the same chapter under the title, *"De Casuum Reservatione,"* and understood a reserved case to be not only one in which the sin was reserved *ratione sui* but also one in which the sin was reserved *ratione censurae.* The Council of Trent asserts:

> Verumtamen pie admodum, ne hac ipsa occasione aliquis pereat, in eadem ecclesia Dei custoditum semper fuit, ut nulla sit reservatio in articulo mortis, atque ideo omnes sacerdotes quoslibet poenitentes a quibusvis *peccatis et censuris* absolvere possunt; extra quem articulum sacerdotes cum nihil possint in *casibus reservatis,* id unum poenitentibus persuadere nitantur, ut ad superiores et legitimos judices pro beneficio absolutionis accedant. (Italics not in original text.)[69]

Authors after the Council of Trent also interpreted a reserved case not only as one in which the sin was reserved by reason of itself but also as one wherein the sin was reserved by reason of the attached censure.[70]

---

[66] Canons 2252; 2254.

[67] Canons 900, 3°; 2247, § 2.

[68] Canons 2247, § 2; 2253, 2°.

[69] Sessio XIV, *de poenitentia,* c. 7.

[70] Cf., e.g., Aertnys, *Theologia Moralis juxta Doctrinam S. Alphonsi Mariae de Ligorio* (5. ed., 2 vols. Tornaci: Casterman, 1898), lib. VI, nn. 237, 238. (Hereafter cited as *Theologia Moralis.*) St. Alphonsus, *Theologia Moralis,* lib. VI, nn. 580, 581, 591; Ballerini-Palmieri, *De Sacramento Poenitentiae,* sec. V, c. 2, n. 665; Bonacina, *Opera Omnia* (3 vols., Venetiis, 1687), Vol. III, disp. II, quaest. III, punct. 30, n. 3.

When there was question of the precise manner in which the sin and the censure were reserved in papal and episcopal cases, authors disagreed among themselves. According to St. Alphonsus (1696-1787)[71] and Bonacina (1585-1631),[72] in papal reservations the censures were reserved directly while the sin was reserved indirectly by means of the censure. In reference to papal reservations Suarez (1548-1617), the Salmanticenses (16th-17th cent.) and Sanchez (1550-1610) were of the view that the sin also was reserved immediately and directly.[73] They explained, however, that although the sin was reserved directly, nevertheless when the reservation of the censure ceased the reservation of the sin also ceased, since the sin was reserved because of the censure.[74]

According to the more common opinion, papal cases differed from episcopal cases, when it was a question of sins reserved together with a censure, inasmuch as in the former cases if the censure ceased, the reservation of the sin also ceased, while in the latter cases even if the censure ceased or was not incurred, e.g., because of ignorance, the reservation of the sin remained.[75] D'Annibale (1815-1892) adhered to the less common opinion, allowing for the express contrary intention of the bishop.[76]

B. *Present Legislation*

Under the law of the Code reserved cases are considered to include not only sins reserved *ratione sui* but also sins reserved *ratione censurae*.[77] The Code gives a general definition of the

---

[71] *Theologia Moralis,* lib. VI, n. 581.

[72] *Opera Omnia, loc. cit.*

[73] Suarez, *Opera Omnia* (26 vols., Parisiis, 1856-1866), Vol. XXII, dis. 29, sect. 3, n. 10; Salmanticenses, *Cursus Theologiae Moralis* (6 vols. in 4, Venetiis, 1714-1728), tract. X, c. 13, nn. 4, 5; Sanchez, *Opus Morale in Praecepta Decalogi* (2 vols. in 1, Parmae, 1723), lib. II, c. 8, n. 5.

[74] Suarez, *loc. cit.;* Salmanticenses, *loc. cit.;* Sanchez, *loc. cit.*

[75] Cf., e.g., St. Alphonsus, *loc. cit.;* Ballerini-Palmieri, *loc. cit.;* La Croix, *Theologia Moralis* (2 vols., Venetiis, 1722), VI, n. 1614; Craisson, *Manuale Totius Juris Canonici* (5. ed., 4 vols., Pictavii, 1877), lib. III, n. 6480.

[76] *Summula Theologiae Moralis,* I, n. 340.

[77] Cf., e.g., Augustine, *A Commentary on the New Code of Canon Law* (8 vols., Vol. VIII, 1922: *Penal Code,* St. Louis: Herder), VIII, 131-139.

power of reserving cases and includes both the reservation of sins and the reservation of censures.[78] After the Code includes both the reservation of sins and the reservation of censures under the genus of the reservation of cases, specific mention is made of the fact that the reservation of censures is to be governed by separate and distinct canons.[79]

The general heading of the chapter which deals with the definition of the power of reservation is: *De reservatione peccatorum.* The reservation of censures is excluded from the rules legislated in canons 894-900. The first canon which determines the rules governing the reservation of sins states that there is only one sin reserved *ratione sui.*[80] It is in the fifth book that the Code speaks of sins reserved *ratione censurae.*

The term *"casus,"* without any further modification is employed by canon 2249, § 2 to signify cases reserved *ratione censurae* only.[81] Outside of the above mentioned canons contained in the chapters which deal respectively with the reservation of sins and

---

(Hereafter cited as *Commentary.*) Dargin, *Reserved Cases,* p. 5; Farrugia, *De Casuum Conscientiae Reservatione,* pp. 13, 14; Marc-Gestermann-Raus, *Institutiones,* II, nn. 1766, 1771; Noldin-Schmitt, *Summa Theologiae Moralis,* III, pp. 362-368; Shuhler, *Privileges of Regulars to Absolve and Dispense,* The Catholic University of America Canon Law Studies, n. 186 (Washington, D. C.: The Catholic University of America Press, 1943), pp. 67-70.

[78] Canon 893, § 1. Qui ordinario iure possunt audiendi confessiones potestatem concedere aut ferre censuras, possunt quoque . . . nonnullos casus ad suum avocare iudicium. . . . The second paragraph of the same canon states: "Haec *avocatio* dicitur reservatio casuum."

Cf. *infra,* p. ??

[79] Canon 893, § 3. Quod attinet ad reservationem censurarum, servetur praescriptum can. 2246, 2247.

[80] Canon 894.—Unicum peccatum *ratione sui* reservatum Sanctae Sedi est falsa delatio, qua sacerdos innocens accusatur de crimine sollicitationis apud iudices ecclesiasticos. (Italics not in original text.)

In the following canons the rules concern the local Ordinary and religious superiors who reserve sins *ratione sui.*

[81] Canon 2249, § 2. Petens absolutionem, debet *casus* omnes indicare, secus absolutio valet tantum pro *casu* expresso; quod si absolutio, quamvis particularis petitio facta sit, fuerit generalis, valet quoque pro reticitis bona fide, excepta censura specialissimo modo Sedi Apostolicae reservata, non autem pro reticitis mala fide. (Italics not in the original text.)

censures in general the phrase "*casus reservatus*" is found, e.g., in canons 349, § 1, 1°;[82] 883;[83] 274, 5°[84] and 518, § 1.[85] In these canons the Code refers to both reserved sins and censures. Under these reserved censures, however, are not included *ab homine* reserved censures.

In other canons the code explicitly mentions both reserved sins and reserved censures.[86]

C. *Comparison of Papal and Episcopal Cases*

The distinction which was made by pre-Code authors and was considered the common opinion is the following: in papal reserved censures the censure was reserved primarily and the sin was reserved only because of the censure, while in episcopal censures the sin was reserved principally and the censure was reserved accessorily. After the Code, however, the majority of authors rejects this distinction and maintains that in all cases reserved *ratione censurae,* whether by law the case is reserved to the Holy See or to the bishop, even in cases in which the latter reserves

[82] Can. 349, § 1, 1°. Praeter alia privilegia quae suis in titulis recensentur, fruuntur privilegiis de quibus in can. 239, § 1, nn. 7-12; nec non n. 2, etiam quod spectat ad casus Ordinario loci reservatos. . . .

[83] Canon 883, § 2. Quoties vero navis in itinere consistat, possunt confessiones excipere tum fidelium qui quavis de causa ad navim accedant, tum eorum qui ipsis ad terram obitur appellantibus confiteri petant eosque valide ac licite absolvere etiam a casibus Ordinario loci reservatis.

[84] Canon 274, 5° . . . tempore autem visitationis, potest praedicare, confessiones audire etiam absolvendo a casibus Episcopo reservatis.

[85] Canon 518, § 1. In singulis religionis clericalis domibus deputentur plures pro sodalium numero confessarii legitime approbati, cum potestate, si agatur de religione exempta, absolvendi etiam a casibus in religione reservatis. Compare with canon 519.

[86] Cf., e.g., canon 239, § 1 . . . Cardinales omnes a sua promotione in consistorio facultate gaudent:

2°: Sibi suisque familiaribus eligendi sacerdotem confessionibus excipiendis, qui si iurisdictione careat, eam ipso iure obtinet, etiam quod spectat *ad peccata et censuras, reservatas* quoque, illis tantum censuris exceptis, de quibus in n. 1. . . .

Canon 519 . . . confessarius potest religiosum absolvere etiam *a peccatis et censuris* in religione *reservatis.* (Italics not in the original text.)

a censure to himself, the censure is reserved principally and the sin is reserved accessorily or only *ratione censurae.* The distinction which in the old law was made between cases reserved *ratione censurae* to the Pope and cases reserved *ratione censurae* to the bishop can be considered no longer in force. Even though the bishop wished to reserve a sin and censure *aeque principaliter,* he no longer can do so.[87]

Prümmer[88] and Marc-Gestermann-Raus hold the opposite opinion.[89] Marc-Gestermann-Raus allege as a confirmation of this point of view the universal practice of bishops in reserving cases to themselves. But, as they admit,[90] one has to consider in particular the intention of the bishop. Practically, then, one will have to inquire in every case whether the bishop intends to reserve the sin and the censure principally or the censure principally and the sin accessorily, if the opinion which he proposes is to be followed. The Code, however, neither confirms nor implies any distinction between those cases which the Pope reserves *ratione censurae* to himself and those cases which the bishops reserve to themselves with a censure. One can, therefore, rightly conclude that the distinction no longer exists.[91]

---

[87] Canon 2246, § 3. Cf. Cappello, *De Censuris,* n. 70, 3°; Chelodi, *Ius Poenale,* p. 39, note 2; Cocchi, *Commentarium in Codicem Iuris Canonici* (2. ed., 8 vols., Taurinorum Augustae: Marietti, 1922-1930; Vol. VIII, *De Delictis et Poenis,* 4. ed., 1938), VIII, 110; Coronata, *Institutiones Iuris Canonici,* IV, 161; Genicot-Salsmans, *Institutiones Theologiae Moralis* (10. ed., 2 vols., Bruxellis, 1922), II, n. 344; Noldin-Schmitt, *Summa Theologiae Moralis,* III, n. 363, 3°; Salucci, *Il Diritto Penale secondo il Codice di Diritto Canonico* (2 vols. in 1, Subiaco: Typografia dei Monasteri, Vol. I, 1926; Vol. II, 1930), p. 204, note 2. (Hereafter cited as *Diritto Penale.*) Sole, *De Delictis et Poenis,* n. 174; Sipos, *Enchiridion,* p. 918.

[88] *Manuale Theologiae Moralis secundum Principia S. Thomae Aquinatis* (4. and 5. ed., 3 vols., Friburgi Brisgoviae, 1928), III, 423, 419-427. (Hereafter cited as *Manuale Theologiae Moralis.*)

[89] *Institutiones,* II, n. 1770. They assert: "Et idem valet quoad casus, quos Episcopi sibi reservant *cum censura,* quia dum in casibus papalibus *censura principaliter reservatur* et secundario peccatum, e contrario, in casibus episcopalibus, *principaliter et per se reservatur ipse casus,* seu peccatum, etiam quando accessorie, ad fortius ligandum, annexa est censura."

[90] *Institutiones,* III, 306, note 1.

[91] Cf. Canons 2245, §§ 2-3; 2246, § 1, § 3; 2250, § 2. These canons speak of censures reserved to the Holy See or to the bishop in general, and apply the same principles to both kinds of reservations.

According to some authors, the term *"casus papales"* refers, not only to those cases which are reserved to the Pope by the common law, but also to those cases which are reserved by the common law to local ordinaries; the term *"casus episcopalis"* refers to those cases which the bishop reserves to himself outside of the cases reserved to him by the common law.[92] Raus asserts that a simple confessor who has faculties to absolve from cases reserved to the Roman Pontiff, can also absolve from censures reserved to the ordinary by the Code, since these censures are papal cases.[93]

Marc-Gestermann-Raus, Blat, Prümmer and Kane, however, have a different concept of papal and episcopal cases. Marc-Gestermann-Raus include under papal cases only those cases which are reserved to the Pope either because of the sin (*ratione peccati*) or because of a censure reserved in any one of the three ways, i.e., *specialissimo modo, simplici modo* or *simpliciter,* and under episcopal cases those cases which are reserved to the bishop either *a iure communi* or *ab homine.*[94] Those cases, they say, are reserved *ab homine* to the bishop which the bishop either in the Synod or outside of the Synod by way of general legislation reserves to himself, and ordinarily without any censure attached.

---

[92] Cf. Coronata, *Institutiones Iuris Canonici,* IV, 162; Noldin-Schmitt, *ibid.,* n. 361; Vitali, "De Crimine Occulto Abortus, Deque Facultate ab Eodem, Tempore Quoque Iubilaei Maximi, Absolvendi,"—*American Ecclesiastical Review (Ecclesiastical Review, The* [originally *The American Ecclesiastical Review*], Philadelphia, 1889-), LXXIII (1925), 283. (Hereafter cited as *AER.*) Vitali, also "De Reservationibus Pontificiis A Jure Reservatis Ordinario deque Regularium *Privilegio ab Iisdem Absolvendi,"—Commentarium pro Religiosis* (Romae, 1920-; ab anno 1935, *Commentarium pro Religiosis et Missionariis*), XIV (1933), p. 289. (Hereafter cited as *CpR.*) Farrugia (*ibid.,* pp. 14, 15) under papal cases includes censures or sins reserved to the Holy See and under episcopal cases includes censures and sins reserved generally without a censure attached which the bishop reserves to himself. He does not classify censures reserved to the bishop by the common law.

[93] Raus, *Institutiones Canonicae juxta Novum Codicem Juris pro Scholis vel ad Usum Privatum Synthetice Redactae* (ed. altera, Lugduni, Parisiis, 1931), p. 697 and p. 697, note 5.

[94] *Institutiones,* III, nn. 1771, 1772. Cf. also Prümmer, *Manuale Theologiae Moralis,* III, nn. 421, 427.

In a similar manner Blat considers that a case is papal when the limitation of jurisdiction in relation to the absolution from those cases affects the power of all superiors who are inferior to the Pope, and that a case is episcopal when the limitation of jurisdiction does not affect the power of bishops or other similar prelates.[95] In the latter category, therefore, are included all cases reserved to the bishop either by the common law or by the bishop himself. He further distinguishes cases which are to be considered either *a iure communi* or *ab homine.* In the first category he places all cases reserved by the Holy See either to the Holy See itself or to the bishops; in the second category he places all cases reserved by prelates themselves who are inferior to the Roman Pontiff.[96]

Kane, who does not formally define what his concept of a papal reserved case is, nevertheless uses the term "papal reserved case" to refer to censures (cases) which are reserved to the Pope and not to the bishop by the common law. He writes:

> In the response given 21 December, 1899, the Sacred Penitentiary seems to have gone beyond the scope of the *dubium,* and to have made a sweeping declaration that this suspension of faculties does not affect those penitents who at the time of confession, in the judgment of the Ordinary or the confessor, can not here and now go to Rome. As this would be the condition of practically any penitent in this country, it would seem that a Regular could generally make use of his faculties for absolving from Papal reserved cases.[97]

The Code itself does not make a formal distinction between *casus papales* and *casus episcopales.* The Code uses the term "casus" three times in reference to the reservation of sins *ratione sui* in Book III, Part I, Title IV, Chapter II,[98] and twice in

[95] *De Rebus,* Pars I, p. 258. Cf. also Lega, *De Delictis et Poenis,* p. 199, note 1.

[96] *Loc. cit.*

[97] "Suspension of Faculties from Absolving from Cases Reserved to Ordinaries"—*AER,* LXXII (1925), 401.

[98] Canon 897.—*Casus* reservandi sint pauci omnino. . . .

Canon 899, § 3. Ipso iure a *casibus,* quos quoquo modo sibi Ordinarii

reference to the reservation of cases in general.[99] At other times the Code states that the sin is reserved *ratione sui*[100] or *ratione censurae,*[101] or that a certain censure is reserved either to the Holy See, to the Ordinary or to no one.[102] To avoid misunderstandings it is best to use the terminology employed by the Code.

---

reservaverint, absolvere possunt tum parochi, aliive qui parochorum nomine in iure censentur. . . .

Canon 900, 2° . . . Quoties vel legitimus Superior petitam pro aliquo determinato *casu* absolvendi facultatem denegaverit. . . . (Italics not in original text.)

[99] Canon 893, § 1, § 2. Cf. also *supra,* pp. ??.

[100] Canon 894.

[101] Canon 898.

[102] E.g., canons 2314, § 2; 2318, § 1, § 2; 2319, § 1; 2352.

CHAPTER III

The Power of Reserving Censures

ARTICLE I. THE AUTHOR OF RESERVATION

In general, those are invested with the power to reserve censures who possess the power to inflict or enact censures.[1] The power to enact censures is an act of jurisdiction, and specifically an act belonging to the external forum.[2]

The following physical persons have the power (limited or unlimited) to enact or inflict censures and as a consequence have the power to reserve to themselves absolution from these censures:[3]

1. The Roman Pontiff who can reserve censures to himself or to other superiors, and whose jurisdiction extends to all the faithful, even to bishops, legates and cardinals taken either individually or collectively;[4]

2. bishops in the diocesan synod by way of law or outside the synod by way of statute;[5]

3. a cardinal promoted to a suburbicarian bishopric who has taken canonical possession of the diocese, but not other cardinals;[6]

4. metropolitans during the visitation only or whenever there

---

[1] Canon 893; cf. also, Cappello, *De Censuris,* n. 66; Coronata, *Institutiones Iuris Canonici,* IV, 83, 162. The term, "inflict" does not refer to the mere application of a penalty.

[2] Canon 2221. Cf. Cappello, *ibid.,* n. 10.

[3] For general reference cf. Cappello, *ibid.,* n. 11; Chelodi, *Ius Poenale,* n. 24; Coronata, *loc. cit.*; Cipollini, *De Censuris Latae Sententiae iuxta Codicem Iuris Canonici* (Taurini: Marietti, 1925), n. 151; (hereafter cited as *De Censuris Latae Sententiae*). De Meester, *Juris Canonici et Juris Canonico-Civilis Compendium,* III, n. 1711; Farrugia, *De Casuum Conscientiae Reservatione,* pp. 15-19; Marc-Gestermann, *Institutiones,* I, n. 1255; Woywod, *A Practical Commentary,* II, n. 2055.

[4] Canons 218; 219.

[5] Canons 334; 335; 2220; 2221.

[6] Canon 240, §§ 1-2.

is question of appeal from the judicial sentences of the suffragan bishops;[7]

5. the patriarchs of the Oriental Church but not Patriarchs or Primates of the Latin Church;[8]

6. legates *a latere* by delegation only from the Holy See;[9]

7. vicars and prefects apostolic, unless the Holy See reserves the power to itself;[10]

8. administrators apostolic, if they are permanently constituted; if they are temporarily constituted they possess the same authority as a vicar capitular;[11]

9. abbots or prelates *nullius*;[12]

10. vicars capitular;[13]

11. major superiors in exempt religious communities;[14]

12. All to whom special faculties have been delegated either in whole or in part.[15]

The Vicar General can not inflict penalties unless he has a special mandate.[16] The pastor has no jurisdiction in the external forum and therefore cannot enact penalties.[17]

---

[7] Canon 274.

[8] Canons 271; 280.

[9] Canons 266; 267.

[10] Canon 294, § 1.

[11] Canon 315.

[12] Canons 319; 323.

[13] Canons 198; 435; 437.

[14] Canons 198, § 1; 488, 8°; 2220, § 1. The minor local religious superior in clerical exempt religious institutes who has no judicial power can at least apply and reserve, according to canon 2225, the penalties which he himself has constituted but not those penalties which are already constituted in the law. Cf. Clancy, *The Local Religious Superior* (The Catholic University of America Canon Law Studies, n. 175, Washington, D. C.: The Catholic University of America Press, 1943), pp. 196, 197. Roberti ("Quaenam Poenae Applicari Possint per Modum Praecepti,"—*Apollinaris,* IV [1931], 297-299) maintains that any penalty can be inflicted *per modum praecepti* unless a judicial process is required by the legislator.

[15] Canon 199, § 1.

[16] Canon 2220, § 2.

[17] Cf. Ayrinhac-Lydon, *Penal Legislation in the New Code of Canon Law* (revised ed., New York: Benziger, 1936), p. 320 (hereafter cited as *Penal Legislation*). Cappello, *De Censuris,* n. 12; Cipollini, *loc. cit.;* Coronata, *Institutiones Iuris Canonici,* IV, 83; Farrugia, *De Casuum Conscientiae Reservatione,* p. 18.

The following moral persons have the power to inflict penalties for their respective territories:

1. An ecumenical council;[18]
2. plenary and provincial councils;[19]
3. the cathedral chapter before the election of the vicar capitular;[20]
4. chapters of religious orders in accordance with the Code and their constitutions.[21]

According to some authors the Roman Congregations do not possess the power of inflicting penalties unless the Roman Pontiff gives them a mandate, with the exception of the Holy Office which is at the same time a tribunal.[22] According to others the Sacred Congregation can attach penalties to the decrees and precepts which fall under their competency.[23] This latter opinion seems the more probable opinion since canon 2220, § 1, grants the power to inflict penalties to all who possess the right of establishing laws or imposing precepts.[24]

ARTICLE II. THE RESTRICTION OF THE POWER TO ESTABLISH A RESERVATION

A. *Pre-Code Legislation*

Limitations were placed upon the power of bishops to reserve censures. These limitations were related especially to the consideration of the spiritual welfare of souls and also of the preservation of ecclesiastical discipline. The Council of Trent repeatedly set down norms which were to be followed in the use of

[18] Canon 228.

[19] Canons 281; 291.

[20] Canon 435.

[21] Canon 501; cf. Cappello, *loc. cit.;* Chelodi, *loc. cit.;* Cipollini, *loc. cit.*

[22] Canon 247, § 2. Cf. Chelodi, *ibid.*, n. 24, note 1; Salucci, *Diritto Poenale,* p. 102, note 1.

[23] Cappello, *ibid.*, n. 11, note 7; Coronata, *loc. cit.;* Vermeersch-Creusen, III, n. 411. Cf. also canons 2220, § 1; 2221.

[24] Canon 2220, § 1. Qui pollent potestate leges ferendi vel praecepta imponendi, possunt quoque legi vel praecepto poenas adnectere. . . .

censures and their reservation. In session XIII on reform, chapter 1, the Council of Trent decreed that discipline which was so salutary and necessary for the people, should be preserved without harshness and that chastisement should serve the purpose of correction, or, at least that of deterring others from vice. In another place the Council admonished that the reservation of cases should be used unto edification, not unto destruction, especially in regard to those crimes which carried with them the censure of excommunication.[25] In still another place all were warned that excommunications had to be used with moderation and great discretion, since experience taught that in being used rashly or for trifling reasons they produced destruction rather than salvation.[26]

Bishops were prohibited from reserving cases already reserved in the *"Bulla Coenae,"* or also those already specially reserved to the Holy See. This prohibition was issued by the Sacred Congregation of Bishops and Regulars in the year 1602.[27] The reasons were: first, this act of reservation would be superfluous; secondly, as is stated in the letter of the Congregation, there was already hardly a sin remaining which was not reserved;[28] and thirdly, this restriction was needed as a disciplinary measure for the faithful.[29] Although the bishop in his synod could not generally reserve to himself those cases already reserved to the Holy See, nevertheless he could reserve a case concerning the violation of the cloister of exempt nuns, since the bishop was delegated by the Holy See itself to be vigilant concerning the keeping of the law of the cloister.[30]

---

[25] *Sess. XIV, de poenitentia,* c. 7.

[26] *Sess.* XXV, *de ref.,* c. 3.

[27] S. C. Ep. et Reg., litt. 26 nov. 1602—*Codicis Iuris Canonici Fontes cura Emi. Petri Card. Gasparri Editi* (9 vols., Romae postea Civitate Vaticana: Typis Polyglottis Vaticanis, 1923-39, Vols. VII-IX, ed. cura et studio Emi Justiniani Card. Serédi), n. 1615. (Henceforth this work will be cited as *Fontes.*) Cf. also Benedictus XIV, *De Synodo Dioesesana* (2 vols., Venetiis, 1792), lib. V, cap. 4.

[28] *Loc. cit.*

[29] Benedictus XIV, *De Synodo Dioecesana, loc. cit.*

[30] Cf. Pignatelli, *Consultationes Canonicae* (12 vols., Coloniae: Sumptibus Gabrielis et Samuelis De Tournes, 1700-1719), tom. I, consult. 75, n. 1, and consult. 76, n. 1.

The Sacred Congregation of the Propagation of the Faith, in writing to the Vicar Apostolic of Sutchuen, offered a good example of the circumstances which could demand the revocation of reserved cases for the good of the Church.[31] These circumstances were: the remote distance between the missions, the small number of priests, the hardships of the times and the impediments caused by persecutions. In view of all these circumstances a less fruitful exercise of the ministry would have to be expected from those whose jurisdiction was limited by a new reservation of cases.[32]

The Holy Office also warned bishops to be cautious and sparing in the use of penal sanctions to which they wished to attach their reservations, and then repeated the admonition given in the Council of Trent.[33]

B. *Present Legislation*

1. Directive Norms for Ordinaries

The present legislation in harmony with the pre-Code laws clearly states that a censure should not be reserved unless the peculiar gravity of the offense and the necessity of maintaining ecclesiastical discipline and of correcting more effectively the morals of the faithful require it.[34] In a previous canon the legislator warns that censures, especially *latae sententiae* censures, and most of all excommunication, should be inflicted only with moderation and great restraint.[35] The reservation which aggravates the punishment involved in an inflicted censure requires

---

[31] S. C. de Prop. Fide, instr. (ad Vic. Ap. Sutchuen.), 6 iun. 1817, n. 4—*Collectanea S. Congregationis de Propaganda Fide* (2 vols., Romae, ex Typographia Polyglotta Vaticana, 1907), n. 723; *Fontes,* n. 4710.

[32] ". . . ideo Ecclesiae bonum postulat ne plures nunc casus reserventur, quam canonica lex praescribit, et vetus postulat consuetudo. Quare reservationes noviter indictae erunt omnino revocandae."—*Fontes,* n. 4710.

[33] S. C. S. Off., instr. 13 iul. 1916, n. 5—*AAS,* VIII (1916), 314; *Fontes,* n. 1302. Cf. also Conc. Trident., sess. XIV, *de ref.,* c. 3.

[34] Canon 2246, § 1.

[35] Canon 2241, § 2.

for its use a stronger reason than that justifying the inflicting of the censure. The fact, therefore, that a censure is determined for a certain crime does not in itself call for the imposition of a reservation. The norm laid down in canon 2246, § 1, undoubtedly does not affect the validity of the reservation, but is a directive norm for superiors endowed with the power of reserving censures.[36]

Coronata,[37] Chelodi[38] and Augustine[39] consider it advisable for superiors in their enactment of the reservation of censures to ponder the norms of the canons dealing with the reservation of sins. It must be noted, however, that vigilance should be exercised in order that the norms for the reservation of sins be not confused with the norms for the reservations of censures. Chelodi rightly calls the reader's attention to this fact.[40] The separate treatment of the reservation of sins and the reservation of censures by the Code necessitates this precaution.[41]

2. The Cumulation of Reservations

The second restriction upon the power of the Ordinary to reserve censures is indicated in canon 2247, § 1, which prohibits Ordinaries from attaching to the same offense another censure reserved to himself, if that offense is already punishable with a censure reserved to the Apostolic See.[42] The term *"aliam censuram"* should be understood to signify not only another censure of the same species, e.g., an added excommunication in reference to an already existing excommunication, but also another censure

[36] Cf. Coronata, *Institutiones Iuris Canonici,* IV, 164.

[37] *Loc. cit.*

[38] *Ius Poenale,* n. 33.

[39] *Commentary,* VIII, 132.

[40] *Ius Poenale,* n. 33, note 1: "Propter paritatem rationis, sane attentionem meretur etiam hic dispositio can. 895, quamvis de sola *reservatione peccatorum* vigeat: 'Locorum Ordinarii peccata ne reservent, nisi in Synodo dioecesana discussa vel extra Synodum auditis Capitulo cathedrali et aliquot ex prudentioribus et probatioribus suae dioecesis animarum curatoribus.' "

[41] Cf. *supra,* pp. ??.

[42] Canon 2247, § 1. Si censura Sedi Apostolicae reservata sit, Ordinarius nequit aliam censuram sibi reservatam in idem delictum ferre.

of a different species, e.g., any censure such as suspension and interdict in reference to an excommunication.[43] If, despite the prohibition, the Ordinary attaches to a papal reserved censure another censure reserved to himself, the act of the Ordinary is invalid and is not to be sustained.[44] Augustine, on the contrary, teaches that the reservation of the Ordinary made in opposition to the prescripts of the canon in question is valid and is to be sustained.[45] Ayrinhac-Lydon advert to the question, but do not clearly show their position on the matter.[46] Cappello, Chelodi, Cocchi, De Meester, Prümmer and Vermeersch-Creusen do not treat precisely of the question of invalidity.

The strength of the arguments as proposed by various authors for the invalidity of the act of the Ordinary seems great enough to induce both an intrinsic and an extrinsic probability for the opinion. First, whatever the superior reserves to his judgment is thereby removed from the jurisdiction of inferiors, and, secondly, the Holy See by determining a reservation has a *ius praeventionis*.[47]

Many authors state that even if the Ordinary has reserved a censure to himself but later the Holy Father determines a penalty reserved to himself for that same crime, the censure

---

[43] Blat, *Commentarium Textus Codicis Iuris Canonici* (6 vols., Romae, 1920-1927), lib. V, *De Delictis et Poenis* (1924), pp. 103-105 (hereafter cited as *De Delictis et Poenis*). Coronata, *Institutiones Iuris Canonici*, IV, 164; Augustine, *Commentary*, VIII, 134, 135. Augustine (*loc. cit.*) adds that the Ordinary is not prohibited from inflicting a vindicative penalty.

[44] Blat, *loc. cit.;* Coronata, *loc. cit.;* Salucci, *Diritto Penale*, pp. 205, 206; Woywod, *A Practical Commentary*, II, n. 2088. Woywod (*loc. cit.*) says: "It is not certain whether the law of an Ordinary is invalid, . . . it seems, however, that the term, 'nequit' expresses equivalently the nullity of the law of an Ordinary."

[45] *Op. cit., loc. cit.*

[46] *Penal Legislation in the New Code of Canon Law* (revised ed., New York: Benziger, 1936), n. 88. (Hereafter cited as *Penal Legislation.*) Ayrinhac (*loc. cit.*) asserts: "An Ordinary cannot attach a reserved censure to a delinquency which is already punished with censure reserved to the Holy See. Many regard this act as invalid, although 'nequit' is not *per se* invalidating (Can. 2265)."

[47] Cf. Coronata, *loc. cit.;* Blat, *loc. cit.*

and the reservation made by the Ordinary cease immediately.[48] If a censure is reserved *ab homine* to the Holy See, then the power of the Ordinary is restricted in view of the rule of law "qui prior est tempore, potior est iure."[49] If a censure is reserved to the Holy See in any of the ways determined by canon 2245, § 3,[50] then the reservation of the Ordinary would be useless. Although a censure can be multiplied inasmuch as a delinquency is punishable by different superiors,[51] nevertheless it is hard to conceive of an instance in which a superior who is subject to the Roman Pontiff would punish in a more severe manner a delict which the Holy See already has punished in its own manner. In the case of a multiplying of the same censure, the Ordinary by imposing a reservation would either consider the penitent bound by a censure, the while the Holy See considers the penitent worthy of absolution, or he would grant absolution and thereby would act before the Holy See passes judgment about the matter.[52]

The Ordinary, however, may add another censure which is not reserved for a delict which is punishable with a censure reserved to the Holy See.[53] Also, the Ordinary may validly reserve to himself *latae sententiae* censures which are determined by the Code but not reserved by it to anyone,[54] although he ought regularly to abstain from reserving such censures.[55]

If a case is already reserved *ratione censurae* to the Ordinary by the common law, it is obviously useless for the inferior (in this case the Ordinary) to superimpose his own censure on that of the superior (in this case the Pope). The existence of such a mixed reservation is juridically impossible.[56]

---

[48] Cf. Coronata, *loc. cit.;* Sole, *De Delictis et Poenis,* n. 172, note 1; Salucci, *Diritto Penale,* p. 206.

[49] Reg. 54, R. J., in VI°.

[50] Canon 2245, § 3. E reservatis Apostolicae Sedi aliae sunt *reservatae simpliciter,* aliae *speciali modo,* aliae *specialissimo modo.*

[51] Canon 2244, §§ 2, 3.

[52] Cf. Blat, *De Delictis et Poenis,* pp. 103, 104.

[53] Cocchi, *Commentarium in Codicem Iuris Canonici,* VIII, 111; Coronata, *op. cit.,* IV, 165.

[54] Coronata, *loc. cit.;* Salucci, *ibid.,* p. 206.

[55] Coronata, *loc. cit.*

[56] Cf. Shuhler, *Privileges of Regulars to Absolve and Dispense,* p. 107. For pre-Code authors cf. Suarez, *De Poenitentia,* disp. 31, sect. 4, n. 26; D'Annibale, *Summula Theologiae Moralis,* I, n. 339, note 19.

There still remains the mooted question of whether an Ordinary can at least validly reserve to himself *ratione sui* (by reason of the sin alone) a case already reserved *ratione censurae* to Ordinaries by the common law (*iure communi*).[57] Blat[58] and other authors[59] maintain that the local Ordinary can legitimately reserve *ratione peccati* a sin which is reserved *ratione censurae* by the Code to him. The contrary opinion is upheld by Prümmer[60] and Vitali.[61] Since the latter opinion is probable at least from external authority, it can be concluded that absolutions given in virtue of this probable jurisdiction are valid.[62]

Another question related to the preceding is whether the Ordinary of the place can validly reserve a sin *ratione sui* which is already reserved to the Apostolic See *ratione censurae.* The word *"abstineant"* is employed by the Code when it admonishes local Ordinaries not to reserve *ratione sui* sins which are already reserved *ratione censurae* to the Holy See;[63] while the word *"nequit"* is employed when the Code admonishes all Ordinaries not to inflict another censure reserved to themselves for the same

---

[57] Cf. Coronata, *loc. cit.*

[58] *Commentarium Textus Codicis Iuris Canonici,* III, 265.

[59] Cf. "Consultationes"—*Jus Pontificium* (Romae, 1921-), XIII (1933), 302. (Hereafter abbreviated as *Jus Pont.*) Cf. also anonymous replies to Vitali's opinion and arguments both of which are set forth in *AER,* LXVII (1922), 522; LXXXV (1931), 75-82; LXXXVI (1932), 297-305.

[60] *Manuale Theologiae Moralis* (2.-3. ed., 3 vols., Friburgi Brisgoviae, 1923), III, n. 421.

[61] "Utrum locorum Ordinarii valeant suspendere privilegium Regularium absolvendi a casibus papalibus Ordinariis reservatis 'per accidens et via exceptionis.' "—*AER,* LXXXVI (1932), 292-296. Cf. also the same author's opinion emphatically defended in his other article "De Reservationibus Pontificiis a Jure Reservatis Ordinario deque Regularium Privilegio ab Iisdem Absolvendi,"—*CpR,* XIV (1933), 287-294; 363-375; 436-447; *idem,* "Finis Controversiae circa casus a Iure Reservatos,"—*CpRM,* XVI (1935), 164-175.

[62] Cf. Shuhler, *Privileges of Regulars to Absolve and Dispense,* pp. 107, 108.

[63] Canon 898.—Prorsus ab iis peccatis sibi reservandis omnes abstineant quae iam sint Sedi Apostolicae etiam ratione censurae reservata, et regulariter ab iis quoque quibus censura, etiam nemini reservata, a iure imposita est.

delict for which the Holy See has determined a reserved censure.[64] The question is: do the words *"nequit"* and *"abstineant"* in the two separate canons have an invalidating effect? It has already been demonstrated that the word *"nequit"* very probably connotes an invalidating effect. There remains now the discussion regarding the word *"abstineant."*

In canon 898 the word *"abstineant"* in reference to the second member of the same canon, is doubtlessly not used to denote an invalidating effect, since to abstain *"regulariter"* implies that extraordinarily the Ordinary may reserve *ratione peccati* a sin whose *a iure* attached censure is not reserved. But since in the second member of that canon the distinguishing factor is *"et regulariter,"* the latter implies that the first member of the canon not only refers to the prohibition of *"regulariter"* reserving *ratione sui* what is already reserved to the Holy See *ratione censurae,* but also to the prohibition of reserving even in extraordinary circumstances *ratione sui* what is already reserved to the Holy See *ratione censurae.*

This, as yet, does not prove that the prohibition has an invalidating effect, but it does prove that even extraordinary circumstances do not justify the reserving *ratione sui* of a sin to which is already attached a censure reserved to the Holy See. The strictness of the prohibition and reasons similar to those reasons adduced for the invalidity of the ordinary's enactment which undertakes to correct a reserved censure with a delict which already has attached to it a censure reserved to the Holy See—these two factors together seem to point to the juridical invalidity of any act which constitutes a substantial infraction of the prohibitive legislation.[65] It would seem extravagant if not also preposterous, to acknowledge that a bishop could reserve to himself the absolution of a sin regarding which, because of the

---

[64] Canon 2247, § 1. Si censura Sedi Apostolicae reservata sit, Ordinarius *nequit* aliam censuram sibi reservatam in idem delictum ferre. (Italics not in the original text.)

[65] Cf. Cappello, *De Poenitentia* (Romae: Marietti, 1938), n. 519; Noldin-Schmitt, *Theologiae Moralis,* III, n. 359; Vitali, "De Reservationibus Pontificis a Jure Reservatis Ordinario deque Regularium Privilegio ab Iisdem Absolvendi,"—*CpR,* XIV (1933), 288, 289; Farrugia, *De Casuum Conscientiae Reservatione,* p. 23.

attached censure which reserves its absolution to the Holy See, he himself has no power to grant absolution apart from the delegation to him of such power by the Holy See.[66] This argument has application only in such instances wherein the censure which is reserved to the Holy See constitutes either a public case or, as a secret case, involves a reservation of the censure *specialissimo* or *speciali modo*. For all secret cases which involve a censure which is reserved to the Holy See *simpliciter* only the ordinary has, by the law of canon 2237, § 2, full power to grant absolution. Thus the argument of Noldin-Schmitt must of course be understood within the limitations of its potential application.

A. *Territorial Limitation in General*

When a reserved censure is imposed by the Holy Father or by an ecumenical council or by the Code with the purpose of binding all subjects or particular subjects *toto orbe terrarum,* then there can be no question of the territorial limitation of such reservations. These reservations, imposed by the supreme authority, bind the penitent everywhere. Censures which are inflicted *ab homine* have the same binding effect, namely, they are reserved everywhere, so that the penitent cannot be absolved without the required special faculties.[67]

In determining the territorial limitation of reservations, the Code asserts that only the reservation of a censure which is determined in and for some particular territory has no force outside the limits of that territory, but that this is true even though the person who has incurred the reserved censure leaves the territory precisely to obtain absolution.[68] The reservation of such a censure, therefore, has no force outside the territory of the one reserving; the censure, however, once incurred binds the person everywhere.[69]

[66] Noldin-Schmitt, *loc. cit.*

[67] Canon 2247, § 2 . . . censura vero ab homine est ubique locorum reservata ita ut censuratus nullibi absolvi sine debitis facultatibus possit.

[68] Canon 2247, § 2. Reservatio censurae in particulari territorio vim suam extra illius territorii fines non exserit, etiamsi censuratus ad absolutionem obtinendam e territorio egrediatur. . . .

[69] Canon 2226, § 4. Poena reum ubique terrarum tenet, etiam resoluto iure Superioris, nisi aliud expresse caveatur.

Cf. Ayrinhac, *Penal Legislation,* p. 66; Coronata, *Institutiones Iuris Canonici,* IV, 167.

The reservation itself ceases, so that any confessor may absolve from the censure, but the necessary requisite for the cessation of the censure is absolution.[70]

The Code asserts that the reservation of a censure *in particulari territorio* ceases outside the territory. This phrase is used, according to Blat,[71] to exclude from falling under this rule any censure which has been enacted as a reserved censure for a particular territory by the Pope or an Ecumenical Council. For, he argues, a *latae sententiae* reserved censure which is determined by the ordinary or a council, excluding an ecumenical council, is properly said to be legislated *"in territorio,"* while a particular reservation determined by the Pope or an ecumenical council is properly said to be legislated *"pro particulari territorio."*[72] Since the Code makes no such distinction, it is better to apply the general principles laid down in canon 2247, § 2, to all particular reservations, including those which are determined through a particular law by the Pope or an ecumenical council for a particular territory, and to consider such censures non-reserved outside of the specified territory, unless, of course, the contrary be explicitly stated.[73]

The rule, therefore, that the reservation of a censure determined for a particular territory has no force outside the particular territory may be considered universal.[74] Cappello, however, makes an exception to this rule in regard to prelates of exempt clerical communities,[75] and Coronata agrees with him.[76] Cappello states that the jurisdiction of prelates of exempt clerical communities is a personal jurisdiction over their proper subjects.[77] Consequently, if the religious confessor has confessional faculties only from the religious ordinary, he could not absolve from censures reserved

---

[70] Canon 2248, § 1. Quaelibet censura, semel contracta, tollitur tantum legitima absolutione.

[71] *De Delictis et Poenis*, p. 104.

[72] *De Delictis et Poenis, loc. cit.*

[73] Cappello, *De Censuris*, n. 67; Coronata, *Institutiones Iuris Canonici*, IV, 166-167.

[74] Cappello, *loc. cit.*

[75] *Loc. cit.*

[76] *Op. cit.*, IV, 166.

[77] *Loc. cit.* Cf. also Genicot-Salsmans, *Institutiones Theologiae Moralis*, II, n. 567.

by the same religious ordinary in the community. But, if the religious confessor has faculties also from the ordinary of the place, he may absolve from sins and censures reserved in the community. The canon which deals with the confessions of religious, even exempt, states that a reservation (*a iure,* of course) determined by the prelate is not binding either in the community or outside the community, if the confessor has faculties from the ordinary of the place.[78] Therefore, the reservation of censures determined by religious ordinaries can not be restricted by territorial limits, inasmuch as the jurisdiction of prelates of exempt clerical communities is a personal jurisdiction over their subjects. If, however, the confessor has faculties from the ordinary of the place, then the reservation made for the community ceases.

The reservation of a censure in some particular territory has no force in limiting the jurisdiction of confessors for the internal forum or the jurisdiction of others for the external forum, *extra illius territorii fines,* not inasmuch as those absolving receive jurisdiction from the superior who reserves the censure, but inasmuch as the reservation ceases *a iure communi* outside of the territory of the one reserving.[79]

B. *Reservation of Censures and the* "PEREGRINUS"

1. Historical Notes

In general, censures were considered to participate in the qualities of both local and personal punitive legislation.[80] A *peregrinus* was not affected by the censures of his own diocese. If, therefore, the censure was instituted in his diocese for a certain crime, the subject did not contract either the censure or the

[78] Canon 519 . . . si religiosus, etiam exemptus, ad suae conscientiae quietem, confessarium adeat ab Ordinario loci approbatum, etsi inter designatos non recensitum, confessio, revocato quolibet contrario privilegio, valida et licita est; et confessarius potest religiosum absolvere etiam a peccatis et censuris in religione reservatis.

[79] Cf. Blat, *De Delictis et Poenis,* p. 104; Ayrinhac, *Penal Legislation,* p. 66.

[80] Santi, *Praelectiones Juris Canonici juxta ordinem Decretalium Gregorii IX* (5 vols. in 3, Ratisbon, 1886), lib. V, tit. 39, n. 17.

reservation while he sojourned in another diocese;[81] if the censure was of a *ferendae sententiae* character the bishop himself while absent from his own diocese could not inflict the censure, regardless of the fact that the subject was present in his diocese.[82] The rule as stated for the first case obtained when the censure was reserved by a general statute or sentence, but not when the bishop imposed upon a subject the obligation of obeying a precept with a reserved censure annexed, for then the subject was bound by the reservation even though he was absent from the diocese.[83]

The question of whether a traveler was bound by the reserved censures of the place in which he happened to stay was solved by the authors in accordance with whether he was bound by the laws of the diocese in which he sojourned. The traveler was not bound by the censures, nor in consequence by the reservations, determined by the law enacted for the entire diocese in which he was staying,[84] but by reason of a crime he could be cited to the forum of the place,[85] or a reserved censure could be inflicted by precept.[86]

Suarez agreed that a *peregrinus* did not incur any censure determined by a particular or general sentence, since these sentences bound only subjects, but he maintained that a *peregrinus* was bound by the statutes or general customs through which censures were locally inflicted, for such statutory and customary laws were of a territorial nature and bound all who were present in the territory.[87] St. Alphonsus (1696-1787) distinguished between the reserved case and the excommunication attached to it, and

---

[81] Schmalzgrueber, *Jus Ecclesiasticum Universum* (5 vols. in 12, Romae, 1843-1845), lib. V, tit. 39, n. 49; Suarez, *Opera Omnia*, Vol. XXIII, disp. V, sect. 4, n. 4; Ballerini-Palmieri, *Opus Theologicum Morale*, X, sect. 5, C. 2, n. 735; Santi, *loc. cit.*

[82] Santi, *loc. cit.*; Bucceroni, *Institutiones Theologiae Moralis*, II, n. 1090.

[83] Schmalzgrueber, *loc. cit.;* Ballerini-Palmieri, *loc. cit.;* cf. also Suarez, *ibid.*, disp. V, sect. 5, n. 5; Bucceroni, *Institutiones Theologiae Moralis*, II, n. 1091.

[84] Ballerini-Palmieri, *ibid.*, n. 736. They stated this as a common opinion. Cf. also Suarez, *Opera Omnia*, Vol. XXIII, disp. VII, sect. 2, n. 27.

[85] Santi, *loc. cit.;* cf. also Bucceroni, *Institutiones Theologiae Moralis*, Vol. II, n. 1092.

[86] Suarez, *loc. cit.;* Ballerini-Palmieri, *ibid.*, n. 741.

[87] *Opera Omnia*, Vol. XXIII, disp. 5, sect. 5, nn. 7, 8, 10, 15.

consequently maintained that through his sin the traveler incurred the reserved case, but not the censure.[88] The reason alleged by him was the following: an excommunication is determined for subjects only, whether it be enacted by means of a particular sentence or a general statute.[89] Some authors, then, considered the statutes of a diocese as binding all who were present in the territory for which they were legislated, while others rightly maintained that excommunications enacted by statutes bound subjects only.

If, however, the *peregrinus* had incurred a reserved censure in his own diocese, he could not be absolved in another diocese, even though the censure was not reserved in this other diocese.[90] Absolution from a censure enacted by a general sentence in one's original diocese could be granted by the ordinary of the place to which the penitent had changed his domicile.[91] If, however, there was a question of a censure inflicted by a specific sentence, the opposite solution held regardless of the change of domicile.[92]

In occult cases reserved to the Holy See a *peregrinus* could be absolved by the bishop of the place, but only in the sacrament of penance, by reason of the faculties granted by the Council of Trent.[93] The term *"suos subditos"* was therefore interpreted in the general sense, inasmuch as the bishop's jurisdiction extended also to those who became incidentally subject to him at least by tacit delegation.[94] This faculty could be delegated generally, ac-

[88] *Theologia Moralis,* lib. VI, n. 591; cf. also Salmanticenses, *Cursus Theologiae Moralis* (6 vols. in 4, Venetiis, 1714-1728), tract. X, C. 1, n. 117.

[89] St. Alphonsus, *loc. cit.;* cf. also Salmanticenses, *ibid.,* nn. 116, 117.

[90] St. Alphonsus, *Theologiae Moralis,* lib. VI, n. 590; Ojetti, *Synopsis,* p. 454; St. Alphonsus and Ballerini (1805-1881) were of the opinion that a *peregrinus* could be absolved by any confessor, even by one not having faculties for absolving from any reserved sins committed in the former's diocese, as long as he did not leave it *in fraudem reservationis*—Ballerini, *ibid.,* n. 742; St. Alphonsus, *ibid.,* n. 589; cf. also Bucceroni, n. 797; D'Annibale, *Manuale Theologiae Moralis,* III, n. 322.

[91] Suarez, *Opera Omnia,* Vol. XXIII, disp. 7, sec. 2, n. 26.

[92] Suarez, *loc. cit.*

[93] Sess. XXXV, *de ref.,* c. 6. Cf. Suarez, *Opera Omnia,* Vol. XXIII, disp. XLI, sec. 2, n. 12; St. Alphonsus, *ibid.,* n. 593; Ballerini, *ibid.,* n. 740; D'Annibale, *Summula Theologiae Moralis,* III, n. 346.

[94] Ballerini, *loc. cit.*

cording to the most common opinion,[95] since it was an ordinary power which was annexed to his office and granted by the common law.

The question was proposed by St. Alphonsus whether or not bishops could absolve from occult cases when such cases were reserved by other bishops even with a censure.[96] At first he asserted that the affirmative opinion was probable, but later he held the negative opinion. Commenting on St. Alphonsus' change of opinion, Ballerini (1805-1881), maintained that a bishop could absolve a *peregrinus* who had left his diocese not *in fraudem reservationis,* all the more so since an ordinary confessor had the power to do so, a fact which even St. Alphonsus admitted; if, on the other hand, a bishop was only visiting in another diocese, then the ordinary of the place could surely limit the faculties granted to the visiting bishop in relation to the cases reserved to himself.[97]

2. Present Legislation

In the present legislation a censured person can absent himself from the territory of the superior who determined the reservation even for the sole purpose of obtaining absolution. The rule, therefore, *"fraus et dolus memini patrocinari debent,"* and the clause *"nisi in fraudem reservationis egerit,"* can not be applied to canon 2247, § 2.[98] Further, the jurisdiction to absolve the *peregrinus* from *a iure particulari* determined and incurred censures reserved in his own particular territory is not implicitly granted by the ordinary of the *peregrinus.* The reservation has no force outside of the territory of the one reserving and consequently jurisdiction is granted by the common law.[99]

---

[95] St. Alphonsus, *ibid.,* n. 594, dub. 9; Ballerini, *loc. cit.* Both authors conclude that, if the bishop himself had incurred such a censure, he could give faculties to his confessor to absolve him.

[96] St. Alphonsus, *ibid.,* n. 594, dub. 8.

[97] *Bullarium Benedicti* XIV, Vol. I, p. 104, 3; Ojetti, *loc. cit.*

[98] Cf. Blat, *De Delictis et Poenis,* p. 104.

[99] Cf. *supra,* p. 55 and canon 2247, § 2. A *vagus* who because of canon 14, § 2 incurs a censure reserved in a particular territory because of canon 2247, § 2 can be absolved by any confessor while he is absent from that particular territory in which the censure is reserved.

In a comparative study of the reservation of sins and the reservation of censures, the answers to the following two questions will give a clear concept of the difference of jurisdictional limitations: 1. Is a subject of diocese A, who happens to be present in diocese B and confesses a sin which was committed in diocese A and is only reserved in diocese B, bound by the reservation? 2. Is a subject of diocese A, who incurs a censure reserved *a iure* by diocesan statute and then leaves his diocese to obtain absolution in diocese B, where there exists a like diocesan reserved censure, bound by the reservation of the censure in diocese B?[100] The answer to the first question is in the affirmative, because the confessor's jurisdiction is limited. This conclusion is in full agreement with the response made by the Pontifical Commission for the interpretation of the Code, namely, that a *peregrinus* is bound by the reservations of the place in which he is.[101] In reference to this first question there exists no dispute, since the Commission for the Interpretation of the Code replied that the *peregrinus* is bound by the reservations of the place in which he happens to sojourn.[102] In reference to the second question there are authors who maintain that the *peregrinus* is also bound by the reservations of the censures of the place in which he happens to be.[103] The arguments which they propose are not without some foundation; for, they assert, canon 893, §§ 1 and 2, concerning which the Code

---

[100] Canon 14 states that a *peregrinus* is generally not bound by the laws of the territory in which he happens to be. He could incur a reserved censure, if the censure was determined by law for the preservation of the public order. Cf. Van Hove, "La territorialité et la personalité de lois en droit canonique depuis Gratien (vers 1140) jusqu'a a Jean Andreae (✠ 1348)"—Tijdschrift voor Rechtsgeschiedenis; Revue d'histoire du Droit (1922), 309, note 1.

[101] Nov. 24, 1920—*AAS*, XII (1920), 575.

[102] Cf. Coucke, V., "De absolutione a peccatis reservatis,"—*Collationes Brugensis*, XXVIII (1928), 236. Coucke (*loc. cit.*) states that the *peregrinus* can not be absolved by a simple confessor, even if the sin had been committed in another diocese where it was not reserved.

[103] Dargin, *Reserved Cases*, pp. 75, 76; Hammill, *The Obligations of the Traveler according to Canon 14* (The Catholic University of America Canon Law Studies, n. 160, Washington, D. C.: The Catholic University of America Press, 1942), p. 124. (Hereafter cited as *The Obligations of the Traveler.*)

Commission gave its reply, refers to sins reserved by reason of themselves, as well as to sins reserved by reason of censures, and, as a consequence, the interpretation of the Code Commission must apply to reserved censures as well as to reserved sins.[104] Hammill observes that strangers are subject to the reserved censures of the place where they are because of the limitation of the jurisdiction of the confessors who receive their jurisdiction from the ordinary of the place.[105]

At first sight their arguments appear to be convincing, but upon a closer examination of the question the probability of the opposite opinion, namely, that a stranger is bound by the reservation of sins, but not by the reservation of the censures of the place (except in those cases in which he is punished for a crime committed in the place where he happens to sojourn), can not be disregarded. The Code Commission was asked whether under c. 893, §§ 1 and 2, a *peregrinus* is bound by the reservations of the place in which he is, and replied in the affirmative.[106] According to some authors who oppose the opinion of Dargin and Hammill the term *"reservationes"* which is used in the response of the Code Commission refers to the reservation of sins only.[107]

To confirm the probability of this assertion the following facts should be taken into consideration: The title of the chapter under which canon 893, §§ 1 and 2, is found deals with the reservation of sins *ratione sui,* although the canon itself includes the definition not only of sins which are reserved *ratione sui* but also of sins which are reserved *ratione censurae.*[108] The canon primarily and *per se* deals with sins reserved *ratione sui.*

---

[104] Cf. Dargin, *loc. cit.;* Hammill, *loc. cit.*

[105] Hammill, *loc. cit.*

[106] *AAS,* XII (1920), 597.

[107] Cicognani, *Ius Canonicum Primo Studii Anno in Usum Auditorum Excerpta* (2 vols. in 1, Romae, 1925), II, 105. (Hereafter cited as *Ius Canonicum.*) Cf. also Ayrinhac, *Penal Legislation,* p. 66; Sipos, *Enchiridion,* p. 918, note 8.

[108] Canon 893, § 1. Qui ordinario iure possunt audiendi confessiones potestatem concedere aut *ferre censuras,* possunt quoque, excepto Vicario Capitulari et Vicario Generali sine mandato speciali, nonnullos casus ad suum avocare iudicium, inferioribus absolvendi potestatem limitantes. (Italics not in the original text.)

In the chapter of the Code which contains the canon in question the term *"reservationes"* is found only three times and refers to sins reserved *ratione sui.*[109] Then also from certain responses of the Sacred Congregations it is clear that the term "reservations" (*reservationes*) is applied to the reservations of sins, that is, of sins reserved by reason of themselves. The decrees which may be adduced to demonstrate this fact are the following:

> Presbyteri vero latini absolvere non possunt fideles graeco-rutheni ritus *a censuris et casibus reservatis* ab Ordinario graeco-rutheno statutis, absque venia eiusdem. Vicissim idem dicatur de presbyteris graeco-ruthenis quoad *censuras et reservationes* statutas ab Ordinario latini ritus. Ad devitandas vere difficultates, quae frequentiores in praxi occurunt, Ordinariatus *omnes a se reservatos casus,* si qui sint, sibi invicem communicent. (Italics not in the original text.)[110]
>
> Presbyteri vero latini absolvere non possunt fideles graeco-rutheni ritus *a censuris et casibus sibi reservatis* ab Ordinario graeco-rutheno absque venia eiusdem. Vicissim idem dicatur de presbyteris graeco-ruthenis quoad *censuras et reservationes* statutas ab Ordinario latini ritus. (Italics not in the original text.)[111]
>
> Cauti insuper omnino sint et quam maxime parci quod ad poenales sanctiones, excommunicationes praesertim, quibus forte suas *reservationes* communiri velint. (Italics not in the original text.)[112]

---

[109] Canon 899, § 1. Statutis semel *reservationibus* quas vere necessarias aut utiles iudicaverint, curent locorum Ordinarii ut ad subditorum notitiam, quo meliore eis videatur modo, eaedem deducantur, nec facultatem a reservatis absolvendi cuivis et passim impertiant. (Italics not in the original text.)

Canon 895.—Locorum Ordinarii peccata ne reservent, nisi re in Synodo dioecesana discussa, vel extra Synodum auditis Capitulo cathedrali et aliquot ex prudentioribus ac probatioribus suae dioecesis animarum curatoribus, *vera reservationis* necessitas aut utilitas comprobata fuerit.

Canon 900.—*Quaevis reservatio* omni vi careat. . . .

[110] S. C. pro Eccl. Orientali, decr., 1 martii, 1929, art. 31—*AAS,* XXI (1929), 158.

[111] S. C. pro Eccl. Orientali, decr., 24 maii, 1930, art. 36—*AAS,* XXII (1930), 352.

[112] S. C. S. Off., instr. 13 iul. 1916, n. 5—*AAS,* VIII (1916), 314.

According to this interpretation the difference of the wording of the two separate canons which treat of the cessation of the reservation of sins and of the cessation of the reservation of censures outside of the territory becomes significant. Canon 900, 3°, states that the reservation of sins (reserved *ratione sui*) ceases outside of the territory of the one reserving, and not simply outside of the particular territory, as does canon 2247, § 2, which deals with the cessation of the reservation of censures.[113]

The *peregrinus* is not *extra territorium reservantis.* Even though he is in an extraneous diocese on a visit, yet he falls under the jurisdiction of the ordinary of the place who reserves to himself a sin *ratione sui* despite the fact that in his own diocese that sin is not reserved. The reservation of a censure, however, *extra illius territorii fines* does not bind the subject. Although a similar diocesan censure exists in the territory in which the *peregrinus* happens to be, nevertheless he who incurs in his own diocese a censure which is reserved *in particulari territorio* is not bound by the reservation *extra illius territorii fines.* Also, he is not bound by the reservation of the censure of the place in which he sojourns, unless by reason of a crime he is cited to the forum of the place where the crime was committed,[114] or unless by reason of laws which concern the safeguarding of public order or of laws which determine the formalities of actions (for instance, in the matter of contracts), he falls under the jurisdiction of the ordinary of the place and may be punished for any transgressions of these laws.[115]

---

[113] Compare the following two canons: canon 900.—Quaevis reservatio omni vi caret:

3° *Extra territorium reservantis,* etiamsi dumtaxat ad absolutionem obtinendam poenitens ex eo discesserit.

Canon 2247, § 2. Reservatio censurae in particulari territorio vim suam *extra illius territorii fines* non exserit, etiamsi censuratus ad absolutionem obtinendam e territorio egrediatur. . . . (Italics not in the original text.)

[114] Canon 1566, § 1. Ratione delicti reus forum sortitur in loco patrati delicti.

§ 2. Licet post delictum reus e loco discesserit, iudex loci ius habet illum citandi ad comparendum, et sententiam in eum ferendi.

[115] Canon 14, § 1. Peregrini:

1° Non adstringuntur legibus particularibus sui territorii quandiu ab eo

Even Dargin who is of the view that the Code Commission intended to include both the reservation of sins and the reservation of censures under the term *"reservationes loci,"* distinguishes between the source of the jurisdiction to absolve from reserved censures and the source of the jurisdiction to absolve from reserved sins.[116] As he asserts, the source of the confessor's jurisdiction to absolve the *peregrinus* from a censure which is reserved in the diocese of the *peregrinus* is not the ordinary of the place in which he happens to be, but the common law.[117] The source of the confessor's jurisdiction to absolve from a reserved sin is the ordinary of the place in which the confession is heard,[118] and therefore a *peregrinus* who confesses to a priest within a diocese other than his own is absolved by virtue of the jurisdiction delegated to that confessor by the ordinary of the confessor and not of the stranger.

The Code Commission, according to Dargin, by restrictive interpretation places an added restriction on the jurisdiction of the confessor in reference to the absolution from censures which the *peregrinus* has incurred in his own diocese.[119] Were that so, then it would logically follow that, if a person should incur a non-reserved censure in his own diocese, he could then not be absolved while he is visiting in another diocese, where the same censure happens to have a reservation attached to it. No one doubts that the Code Commission can by a restrictive interpretation place further limitations on the jurisdiction of a confessor, but in the face of the present doctrine it may be safely concluded that there does not exist a *dubium iuris*.

To conclude the discussion of this question it can, moreover, be

---

absunt, nisi aut earum transgressio in proprio territorio noceat, aut leges sint personales;

2° Neque legibus territorii in quo versantur, *iis exceptis quae ordini publico consulunt,* vel *actuum solemnia determinant.* . . . (Italics not in the original text.)

[116] *Reserved Cases,* p. 75.

[117] Canon 2253.—Extra mortis periculum possunt absolvere:

1°: A censura non reservata, in foro sacramentali quilibet confessarius; extra forum sacramentale quicumque iurisdictionem in foro externo habeat in reum. . . .

[118] Cf. canon 874, § 1.

[119] *Loc. cit.*

said that even for intrinsic reasons the opinion which asserts that a *peregrinus* is bound only by the reservations of sins reserved *ratione sui* has a more solid foundation and can be considered as the better opinion.

From these rules which govern the cessation of reservations outside of the territory of the one reserving are excepted all censures inflicted *ab homine* which bind the penitent everywhere.[120] The reservation of *ab homine* inflicted censures adheres to the person. Only the one who inflicted the censure or passed judicial sentence, or his superior, or his successor or delegate can confer absolution, even though the penitent has acquired a new domicile or quasi-domicile.[121]

An indirect subjection of the *peregrinus* occurs in the infliction of a local interdict.[122] The inflicting of a local interdict, just as the prohibition of residence placed upon a cleric of another diocese for a just cause,[123] is not considered a matter of a particular law, but rather a particular act imposed by the superior.[124] A local interdict directly affects the place and does not oblige outside of the place; but in the interdicted place all, even travelers, and also exempt persons, are indirectly subject to the interdict.

---

[120] Canon 2247, § 2.

[121] Cf. canons 2245, § 2; 2253, 2°.

[122] Canons 2268, § 2; 2269, § 2. Cf. Cappello, *De Censuris*, n. 468; Chelodi, *Ius Poenale*, nn. 39; Hammill, *The Obligations of the Traveler*, p. 124.

[123] Canon 144.

[124] Cf. canon 2269, § 1; Van Hove, "Leges quae ordini publico consulunt,"—*Ephemerides Theologicae Lovanienses* (Brugis, 1924-), I (1924), 158, 159; (hereafter abbreviated as *ETL*). Michiels, *Normae Generales Iuris Canonici* (2 vols., Lublin: Universitas Catholica, 1929), I, 320; Hammill, *ibid.*, p. 125.

CHAPTER IV

The Interpretation and the Extent of the Reservation of Censures

Article I. The Interpretation of the Reservation of Censures

It is clear that in the interpretation of any law, whether favorable or odious, cases which surely exceed the law are not to be included in the law, and that cases which are contained in the law are not to be excluded from the law. In interpreting a law the words can be understood either to signify a more or less general extension. A more general extension of the words of a law would include all the cases which are objectively necessary in order that the end or purpose which is intended by the legislator and which motivated the institution of the law be adequately attained.[1] A less general extension of the words of the law in practice includes those cases which are strictly indicated in the words themselves.[2] Therefore, in the strict interpretation of any law the words of the law are not to be extended to other cases, or persons, but are to be understood literally according to the proper meaning of the words.

A brief consideration of the strict interpretation of penalties themselves will clarify the concept of strict interpretation. In reference to the strict interpretation of penalties Blat states:

> *In poenis . . . benignior,* eo quod 'odia restringi convenit,' ut ait reg. 15 iuris in 6°, *est interpretatio,* cuiuslibet dubii motivo *facienda* semper, tum circa personas, res aut loca sub canone poenali contenta, tum circa delicti conditiones, tum circa poenae acerbitatem, proprietate verborum ceteroquin servata.[3]

[1] Michiels, *Normae Generales,* I, 423, 424.

[2] Michiels, *ibid.,* pp. 430, 431; Cicognani, *Ius Canonicum,* p. 615; Beste, *Introductio in Codicem,* pp. 82-84; Woywod, *A Practical Commentary,* n. 2087.

[3] *De Delictis et Poenis,* p. 54.

Cappello also asserts the necessity of restrictive interpretation as follows:

> Non solum quaelibet interpretatio *extensiva* iure excludenda est in poenalibus, sed *restrictiva* quoque potest ac debet adhiberi, quoties ratio legis eam patitur, quod generatim eruitur ex subiecta materia, ex contextu atque legislatoris intentione.[4]

Although a reservation is not a penalty, still all reservations themselves which are attached to censures are to be interpreted strictly.[5] It will be useful to study the canon which deals with the interpretation of penalties themselves. The canon reads:

> Canon 2219, § 1. In poenis benignior est interpretatio facienda.
>
> § 2. At si dubitetur utrum poena, a Superiore competente inflicta, sit iusta, necne, poena servanda est in utroque foro, excepto casu appellationis in suspensivo.
>
> § 3. Non licet poenam de persona ad personam vel de casu ad casum producere, quamvis par adsit ratio, imo gravior, salvo tamen praescripto can. 2231.

The rules of §§ 1 and 3 can be applied by analogy to the interpretation of the reservation of censures.

Reservation is a *res odiosa,* since it limits the faculties of the confessor,[6] and it aggravates the penalty of the censure by rendering the absolution more difficult to obtain.[7] Consequently, the reservation of any censure, whether the reservation concerns *a iure* or *ab homine* derived censures,[8] can not be extended either from one person to another or from one case to another, although there would exist an equal, even more serious, reason for the

---

[4] *De Censuris,* n. 46.

[5] 2246, § 2. Reservatio strictam recipit interpretationem. Cf. also Cicognani, *loc. cit.;* Cappello, *De Censuris,* n. 69; Blat, *De Delictis et Poenis,* p. 102; Coronata, *Institutiones Iuris Canonici,* IV, 165; Beste, *ibid.,* p. 904; Woywod, *loc. cit.*

[6] Ayrinhac, *Penal Legislation,* p. 65; Coronata, *loc. cit.;* cf. *supra,* p. ??.

[7] Blat, *loc. cit.;* Coronata, *loc. cit.*

[8] Blat, *loc. cit.*

reservation of the other case. Any law, general or particular, any precept, general or particular, any judicial sentence which constitutes a reservation is to be interpreted strictly, provided that no infraction is made upon the proper meaning of the words.[9] This strict interpretation, however, may not be applied to faculties granted for absolving from a reserved censure, or to the absolution itself from the reserved censure.[10]

If any doubt should arise concerning the fact whether a reservation has been attached to a *latae sententiae* determined censure, the reservation does not bind.[11] This would apply, even though the superior had intended otherwise.[12] The doubt which is being discussed is a positive doubt, and not a mere negative doubt.[13] Whenever a positive doubt arises either on the part of the one absolving or on the part of the one being absolved, or whenever the positive doubt is concerned either with the fact whether there has been constituted a law which enacts a reservation, or with the

---

[9] Blat, *loc. cit.*

[10] Canon 66, § 1. Facultates habituales quae conceduntur vel in perpetuum vel in praefinitum tempus aut certum numerum casuum, accensentur privilegiis praeter ius. . . .

§ 3. Concessa facultas secumfert alias quoque potestates quae ad illius usum sunt necessariae; quare in facultate dispensandi includitur etiam potestas absolvendi a poenis ecclesiasticis, si quae forte obstent, sed ad affectum dumtaxat dispensationis consequendae.

Canon 2249, § 2. Petens absolutionem, debet casus omnes indicare, secus absolutio valet tantum pro casu expresso; quod si absolutio, quamvis particularis petitio facta sit, fuerit generalis, valet quoque pro reticitis bona fide, excepta censura specialissimo modo Sedi Apostolicae reservata, non autem pro reticitis mala fide.

Cf. Blat, *ibid.*, pp. 102, 103.

[11] Canon 2245, § 4 . . . et in dubio sive iuris sive facti reservatio non urget.

[12] Cappello, *De Censuris*, n. 67.

[13] Cappello, *ibid.*, n. 71; Coronata, *Institutiones Iuris Canonici,* IV, 163, note 6. A positive doubt is one in which there is present a serious reason moving one to give assent to a given opinion, but it does not remove all prudent fear of one's being in error. A negative doubt, on the other hand, is one in which such a serious reason is not present to justify one's hesitant view, and consequently it furnishes no solid basis on which a prudent person could rest the determination of his assent to the opinion against which he considers the negative doubt to militate.

meaning of a law whose recognized enactment could imply the sanction of a reservation, then the presence and binding force of such a sanction can not be sustained juridically.[14] Therefore in cases of positive doubt regarding the existence of a reservation, the penitent would not, even *ad cautelam,* have to rceive an absolution under the accompaniment of special faculties for the doubtful reservation on the part of the confessor.[15] If in the course of time the doubt were removed with the result of favoring the existence of the reservation, e.g., by an authentic declaration of the Holy See, yet the penitent would not be obliged to seek another absolution.[16]

ARTICLE II. THE EXTENT OF THE RESERVATION OF CENSURES

A. *Historical Notes*

Before the Code the extension and the reservation of *ab homine* and *a iure* derived censures was disputed among canonists. It will suffice to point out these discrepancies by considering the views of the authors separately.

Devoti (1744-1820) gave a singular division of censures. According to him censures were either of a *ferendae sententiae* character, that is, such as were inflicted by a judge through a sentence, or they were of a *latae sententiae* character, that is, such as were established *a iure* and therefore incurred automatically through the very violation of the law.[17] The first group of censures could be removed only by the judge who inflicted them, or by his suc-

---

[14] Cappello, *loc. cit.* A confessor could, for example, doubt whether a certain case is contained in the faculties which have been granted to him in reference to reservations. In the case of such a doubt he could nevertheless grant absolution, though it be quite certain that the penitent is subject to the reservation. Cf. Coronata, *loc. cit.*

[15] Beste, *Introductio in Codicem,* p. 930; Cappello, *op. cit.;* Coronata, *Institutiones Iuris Canonici,* IV, 163.

[16] Coronata, *loc. cit.;* Sole, *De Delictis et Poenis,* n. 176.

[17] *Institutionum Canonicarum Libri Quattuor* (4 vols. in 2, Romae, 1829), II, 225. In the treatment of *latae sententiae* determined censures he asserts (*loc. cit.*) ". . . a jure ipso infligitur eique locus est ipso facto, nimirum statim ac aliquis crimen admisit, et canonis decreta violavit."

cessor, or his delegate, or his superior. In relation to the second group of censures, a priest had no jurisdiction, if they were reserved to the Pope or to the bishop.

Devoti, therefore, .considered the distinction between *latae sententiae* and *ferendae sententiae* censures an adequate division of censures. In the edition of his work in the year 1883 the same division was still proposed, and many examples of *latae sententiae* determined censures were given. Among the many examples and arguments the following passages added clarity to his concept of censures:

> Nam excommunicatio latae sententiae originem repetit ab ipso Apostolo, cujus haec verba sunt *ad Galat.* 1 *vers.* 9: 'Si quis vobis evangelizaverit, praeter id quod accepistis, anathema sit.' Ergo haereticus non hominis sententia, sed ispo facto anathema est, statim ac doctrinam tradit, quae Pauli doctrinae adversetur.[18]
> Sane adversus christianos, qui idolis sacrificium obtulissent, non propria confessione, non sententia opus fuisse, sed eos *facto ipso* in excommunicatione incidisse. . . .[19]
>
> *Sola praesumptio contra synodi definitionem* satis est, ut quis *anathema marantha* sit. Quid aliud latae sententiae excommunicatio est? Quid dicam de duodecim anathematismis a S. Cyrillo Alexand, adversus Nestorium conscriptis, quos probarunt Ephesini et Chalcedonensis Concilii Patres?[20]

All ferendae sententiae determined censurès which were to be inflicted as a *sententia hominis* required a strict judicial process.[21]

---

[18] *Institutionum Canonicarum Libri Quattuor* (juxta ed. quartam Romanam ad Auctore recognitam et additionibus locupletatam, 2 vols. in 1, Leodii: Dessain, 1883), II, 338.

[19] *Institutionum Canonicarum Libri Quattuor, loc. cit.*

[20] *Ibid.*, p. 339.

[21] Devoti (*ibid.*, p. 337) asserted: ". . . monet (here Devoti is quoting Gerson) excommunicationem latae sententiae hoc efficere, 'Ut absque processu alio judiciali, aut nova constitutione possit judex statim, probato facto, vel confessato, ferre juris sententiam, et eamdem publicare: non sic ubi canones essent solum ferendae sententiae, quoniam monitiones et processus secundum terminos juris praerequirerentur multiplices.' Quod quidem est consentaneum juris disciplinae, quae requirit sententiam, qua crimen declaretur; quoniam in foro externo nemo excommunicatione implicatus haberi potest, nisi prius constet, eum esse reum criminis, cui censura ipso jure adjuncta est.

However, Devoti did not explicitly treat of particular precepts as such, and did not classify them under either category of censures. A *latae sententiae* determined censure which was attached to a particular precept could hardly be placed under his division of *latae sententiae* censures. This would be evident from the words:

> Verum in foro interno nulla requiritur judicis declaratio, sed qui crimen patravit, cui conjuncta censura est, statim coram Deo, cui nota et perspicua sunt omnia, excommunicatus efficitur. Suam enim contumaciam et Ecclesiae contemptus satis aperte declarat, qui peccat *in legem,* a qua scit illico, et *ipso facto* constitutas esse censuras adversus illos, qui ei non obtemperant.[22]

Reiffenstuel (1641-1703) offered the following definition of *a iure* and *ab homine* derived censures:

> a jure illa est, quae per sacros canones, constitutiones, aut decreta, vel futura tanquam jura ecclesiastica imposita semper manet etiam mortuo conditore canonum. Ab homine est, quae a judice, vel praelato ecclesiastico per modum mandati, aut sententiae judicialis fertur.[23]

Reiffenstuel did not explain whether the *ab homine* derived censure which was inflicted through a mandate was derivable from both general and particular mandates (precepts). He considered an *ab homine* censure reserved if the censure was inflicted by a special sentence, but he considered an *ab homine* derived censure as non-reserved if the censure was inflicted through a decree of the bishop or a general sentence, and no mention of reservation had been made.[24]

Schmalzgrueber (1663-1735) gave a similar definition of *a iure* and *ab homine* derived censures. The latter censures were inflicted *a iudice* through a mandate or a judicial sentence.[25] These *ab homine specialiter* inflicted censures were reserved to the

---

[22] *Loc. cit.* (Italics not in the original text.)

[23] *Jus Canonicum Universum* (5 vols. in 7, Parisiis, 1864-1870), lib. V, tit. 39, nn. 45, 46.

[24] *Ibid.*, nn. 242, 246.

[25] *Jus Ecclesiasticum Universum,* lib. V, tit. 39, n. 9.

one who had inflicted them,[26] for, according to Schmalzgrueber, in this instance a special sentence was inflicted upon special persons who had been cited.[27] If, on the other hand, a censure which was of an *ab homine* character had been determined *generaliter,* then it was not reserved. The reason alleged was:

> . . . quia non perturbatur tribunal judicis ferentis censuram cum reus non fuerit nominatim citatus.[28]

Craisson (✠ 1881) did not differ from the preceding authors in his definition of *a iure* and *ab homine* derived censures. In reference to the absolution from *ab homine* derived censures he differed from the preceding authors inasmuch as according to his doctrine an *ab homine* derived censure which was inflicted *per sententiam generalem* but was not reserved was to be considered as on the same basis with an *a iure* derived censure.[29]

This manner of considering general precepts clearly manifested the tendency of the authors to conclude that all *ab homine* derived censures were reserved. The conclusion that all ab homine derived censures without any exception were reserved was made by later authors who classified general precepts under *a iure* determined censures.[30]

Since Wernz (1842-1914) and Lega (1860-1935) had a highly developed notion of the division and reservation of censures, it will be helpful to compare their doctrine with that of the Code. The concept of Wernz concerning *latae* and *ferendae sententiae*

---

[26] *Ibid.,* nn. 85-88.

[27] *Ibid.,* n. 94.

[28] Schmalzgrueber, *loc. cit.* Cf. also De Angelis, *Praelectiones Juris Canonici ad Methodum Decretalium Gregorii IX Exactae* (5 vols., Romae: Desclée, 1908; Vol. IV curavit Nazarenus Gentilini, 1891), IV, 375, 376.

[29] *Manuale Totius Juris Canonici,* IV, n. 6443. Cf. also the moralists: D'Annibale, *Summula Theologiae Moralis,* I, n. 345, note 2; Alphonsus, *Theologia Moralis,* lib. VII, n. 73; Bucceroni, *Institutiones Theologiae Moralis,* II, n. 1101.

[30] Cf., e.g., Wernz, *Ius Decretalium ad usum Praelectionum in Scholis Textus Canonici sive Iuris Decretalium* (6 Vols in 7, Romae-Prati, 1899-1913), VI, n. 146 and n. 175. (Hereafter cited as *Ius Decretalium.*) After the issuance of the present Code this manner of considering general precepts is the usual one, as subdivision 5 of the following section B will show.

derived censures was essentially the same as that now expressed in the Code.[31]

According to Wernz, a *latae sententiae* derived penalty was one which was so determined in the law or precept that it was incurred *ipso facto* by the commission of the delict. Here Wernz was in perfect concordance with the concept later adopted in the Code. But in defining a *ferendae sententiae* derived penalty the Code simply states that the penalty has to be inflicted by a judge or superior, and does not expressly state that it is to be determined either in the law or precept, as Wernz stated in his definition. This, however, is a minor difference, since under the law of the Code censures may be added either to the law or to a precept.

In the definition of censures derived *a iure* there are found two discrepancies between Wernz's view and the law of the Code. Wernz included under *a iure* derived censures those which were determined by way of a true law, either universal or particular, and those also which were determined by way of a general precept which lacked perpetuity; the Code includes only those censures which are determined by way of a law, whether they are of a *latae* or *ferendae sententiae* character.[32] In reference to the reservation of these censures Wernz stated that censures which derived *a iure* were not reserved unless explicit mention of the reservation was made; the Code specifies that reserved censures derived *a iure* are reserved either to the ordinary or to the Holy See,[33] but also states that *latae sententiae* determined censures are not reserved, unless explicit mention of the reservation is made in the law or in the precept.[34] The Code, therefore, explicitly treats both of the reservation of *a iure* reserved censures and of the reservation or non-reservation of *latae sententiae* determined censures. No author whose opinion has been thus far considered spoke of reservation in precisely this manner. Lastly, the definition of an ab homine derived censure and the question of its reservation are treated alike in Wernz and in the Code.

---

[31] Cf. canon 2217, § 1, 2°; Wernz, *Ius Decretalium*, VI, n. 146, ad IV.
[32] Cf. canon 2217, § 1, 3°; Wernz, *ibid.*, n. 146, ad III.
[33] Canon 2245, § 2.
[34] Cf. Canon 2245, § 4; Wernz, *Ius Decretalium*, VI, p. 154, note 16.

What the phrase "*per modum praecepti peculiaris vel particularis*" includes will be discussed in the following chapter.

Lega (1860-1935) included under *ab homine* derived censures all *a iure* derived *ferendae sententiae* censures as well as the censures which were to be considered as deriving strictly and simply *ab homine*. The first category of censures demanded a special condemnatory sentence by a judge, who was always the bishop to whom all criminal causes were reserved. After these censures were inflicted, they became reserved to the judge who had inflicted them, unless the absolution was expressly reserved to the legislator of the law or of the penalty itself. This express manner of reservation on the part of the legislator, Lega said, was not customary. The second category of censures included those which the ordinary of the place by his own authority determined and which because of the transgression of some law or precept were incurred either *ipso facto* or in consequence of a later act through which they were inflicted if they were of a *ferendae sententiae* character.

According to Lega, therefore, a censure was to be considered as deriving *ab homine* if the censure was inflicted either by means of a particular precept, or in consequence of a condemnatory sentence in reference to any censure which, while determined *a iure*, was of a *ferendae sententiae* character. The *cognitio iudicialis* occurred when the censure was declared or when a decision was reached in the decernment of the penalty.[85] Finally, according to Lega's doctrine, *ab homine* derived penalties were subdivisible into those which were of a *ferendae sententiae* character and those which were of a *latae sententiae* character. There now remains no doubt in the Code with reference to censures derived *a iure* if at the same time they are of a *ferendae sententiae* character, for canon 2217, § 1, 3°, definitely states that after the condemnatory sentence these censures are to be considered after the fashion of censures which derive *ab homine*.

Since it is disputed after the Code whether the *latae sententiae* incurred censures which are attached to particular precepts are to

[85] Lega, *De Delictis et Poenis*, I, 105, 106, 175. In reference to *latae sententiae* determined censures which were enacted by a general precept Lega, basing his conclusion on the existence of a *dubium iuris*, states that explicit mention of the reservation must be made.

be considered as deriving *ab homine* or *tamquam a iure,* and since the Code explicitly states that *a iure* derived penalties are either of a *latae* or *ferendae sententiae* character,[36] and then speaks only of *latae* or *ferendae sententiae* derived penalties in reference to particular precepts,[37] without ever explicitly using the term *"latae sententiae"* in connection with penalties which are derived *ab homine,*[38] it becomes impossible to solve the difficulty of a properly harmonized interpretation of *latae sententiae* determined censures immediately. More consideration will have to be given to the question in the following chapter.

Lega termed both the *latae* and the *ferendae sententiae* determined censure which was attached by a local ordinary to either a law or a precept as a *sententia ab homine* and therefore automatically reserved to him who determined the censure.[39] This notion, namely, that even a *latae sententiae* determined censure which was attached to a general or a particular precept was to be considered as an *ab homine* inflicted sentence, is more clearly understood from the following statement of Lega:

> Si vero iudex decernat; nisi hoc facias, eris excommunicatus seu suspensus, quia sententia iam *lata est,* quamvis suspensa in sua executione, pendente conditione, tenet transgressorem, etsi *quoad cetera* subditus esse desierit. Nam hanc sententiam quod spectat, is effugere non valet iudicis auctoritatem; nempe re non integra, siquidem ubi inceptum est iudicium ibi finiri debet. Intelligitur iudicium iam incoeptum et prope finitum quum iudex sententiam iam tulerit censurae, etsi aliqua conditione suspensam: huiusmodi enim sententiae praemittitur cognitio iudicialis ad tramites appositi processus.[40]

Thus far reserved censures have been considered. There remains now the task of giving some attention, by means of a brief

---

[36] Canon 2217, § 1, 3°.

[37] Cf., e.g., canons 2225, 2243, § 2; 2242, § 2.

[38] Cf., e.g., canons 2217, § 1, 3°; 2245, § 2; 2244, § 3; 2247, § 2; 2252; 2253.

[39] *De Delictis et Poenis,* I, 177: "Sententia praeterea *ab homine* dicitur, quum ab Ordinario loci seu a *iudice ipso,* sua auctoritate, editur particularis censura sive haec incurritur *ipso facto,* sive sit *ferendae s.* ob transgressionem alicuius legis aut praecepti."

[40] *Ibid.,* pp. 157, 158.

discussion, to non-reserved censures. However, if the censure was inflicted *a iure* and no mention of reservation was made, then it was considered as not reserved, though as authors after the Council of Trent maintained, jurisdiction in the external forum was required in order to absolve from the non-reserved censure *a iure*.[41] The question arose just how a pastor or an ordinary confessor acquired the necessary jurisdictional power. Different authors explained this question differently.

Schmalzgrueber maintained that this power either was acquired *a iure communi* or was extraordinary.[42] Devoti simply considered it permissible for all priests who possessed the power of administering the sacrament of penance to absolve from all censures which were not reserved either to the Holy See or to the bishop.[43] Pennacchi (1898) stated that non-reserved censures were to be considered *ad instar* of non-reserved sins and thus absolution could be granted by any confessor.[44] Suarez (1548-1617), in treating of this question, asserted that a special concession was not necessary to absolve from non-reserved censures, since *ex iure communi* it was joined with the power of absolving from mortal sins.[45] This same author maintained that if the confessor in bad

---

[41] Pirhing, *Ius Canonicum Nova Methodo Explicatum* (5 vols. in 4, Dilingae, 1674-1678), lib. V, tit. 39, n. 141; Reiffenstuel, *Jus Canonicum Universum*, lib. V, tit. 39, n. 246; Schmalzgrueber, *Jus Ecclesiasticum Universum*, lib. V, tit. 39, n. 96; Devoti, *Institutionum Canonicarum Libri Quattuor*, II, 364.

[42] *Loc. cit.* Pirhing asserted that pastors had no ordinary jurisdiction in the external forum, but that they received this jurisdiction *a iure* as if by delegation, or that they received it by a grant of the Pope inasmuch as such power was often necessary to confer sacramental absolution from sins. This power was then delegated indirectly to assistants to absolve from non-reserved censures. According to Reiffenstuel, the power of the pastor and confessor was confined to the internal forum. If the excommunication was occult, the person absolved could act in the external forum as one who was not excommunicated; but if the excommunication was public then the sacramental absolution was not sufficient for the external forum. Cf. *Ius Canonicum Universum*, lib. V, tit. 39, nn. 247, 248.

[43] *Institutionum Canonicarum Libri Quattuor*, II, 365.

[44] *Commentaria in Constitutionem Apostolicae Sedis* (2 vols., Romae, 1883), II, 61.

[45] *Opera Omnia*, Vol. XXIII, disp. 7, sect. 5, n. 10.

faith inverted the order in absolving from a non-reserved censure (i.e., absolved from the sin first without absolving from the censure), the absolution was nevertheless valid, provided of course that the penitent was properly disposed.[46] This, however, was not so in relation to reserved excommunications, for then the *culpa* was reserved immediately.[47]

If, however, a censure was determined *a iure* and moreover specific mention of its reservation was made, then only the author of the censure, his superior or a delegate of either could absolve. This was the unanimous view of the pre-Code authors.[48] The superior spoken of is the Pope in respect to all; the superior general in respect to his order; the provincial in respect to the superiors of his province, but not the metropolitan in respect to his suffragans, unless there was a question of an appeal or a *querela.*[49]

B. *Present Legislation*

1. Determinate and Indeterminate Censures

The division of censures which the Code gives is different in some respects from the division which pre-Code authors gave. Some of these differences have been pointed out in the immediately preceding pages. There remains to be made a closer study of the division of censures which the code itself presents. The canon which contains the division and canonical concept of the species of penalties in general, and which is to be applied to the division and canonical concept of censures also is the following:

> Canon 2217, § 1. Poena dicitur:
> 1° *Determinata,* si in ipsa lege vel praecepto taxative statuta sit; *indeterminata,* si prudenti arbitrio iudicis vel

[46] *Opera Omnia,* vol. XXII, disp. 29, sect. 2, n. 10.

[47] Suarez, *loc. cit.*

[48] Suarez, *Opera Omnia,* vol. XXIII, disp. 7, sect. 3, n. 1; Pirhing, *ibid.,* n. 142; Reiffenstuel, *ibid.,* n. 249; Schmalzgrueber, *ibid.,* n. 97; Zallinger, *Institutiones Juris Ecclesiastici* (9 vols. in 5, Romae, 1823), lib. V, tit. 39, n. 311.

[49] Reiffenstuel, *ibid.,* n. 244.

> Superioris relicta sit sive praeceptivis sive facultativis verbis;
> 2° *Latae sententiae,* si poena determinata ita sit addita legi vel praecepto ut incurratur ipso facto commissi delicti; *ferendae sententiae,* si a iudice vel Superiore infligi debeat;
> 3° *A iure,* si poena determinata in ipsa lege statuatur, sive latae sententiae sit sive ferendae; *ab homine,* si feratur per modum praecepti peculiaris vel per sententiam iudicialem condemnatoriam, etsi in iure statuta; quare poena ferendae sententiae, legi addita, ante sententiam condemnatoriam est *a iure tantum,* postea *a iure* simul et *ab homine,* sed consideratur tanquam *ab homine.*

All the species of ecclesiastical penalties can be placed either under the category of determinate (or specific) or indeterminate (or general) penalties.[50] The phrase *"in ipsa lege"* is used to point to a law, either universal or particular.[51] The determination of a penalty may originate not only from a law whether universal or particular, but also from a precept.[52] A determinate penalty may be either of a *latae* or *ferendae sententiae* character inasmuch as the penalty which is to be inflicted is determined by the law itself or by the precept.[53] All penalties which are of a *latae sententiae* character must be determinate penalties;[54] penalties which are of a *ferendae sententiae* character may be either determinate[55] or indeterminate.[56] The judge or superior may be ordered by the law to inflict the *ferendae sententiae* determined pnalty,[57] or he may be permitted by it to inflict the *ferendae sententiae* determined penalty.[58] According to Coronata an *ab*

---

[50] Cf. Coronata, *Institutiones Iuris Canonici,* IV, 75.

[51] Coronata, *loc. cit.*

[52] Canon 2217, § 1, 1°. Before the Code Wernz (*Ius Decretalium,* VI, 74) considered that the determination or specification arose solely from a law, and not from a precept.

[53] Blat, *De Delictis et Poenis,* p. 50; Coronata, *ibid.,* p. 76.

[54] Beste, *Introductio in Codicem,* p. 888; Coronata, *loc. cit.;* Vermeersch-Creusen, *Epitome,* III, 404.

[55] Cf., e.g., canons 2315, 2317, 2328.

[56] Cf., e.g., canons 2523; 2329; 2331, § 1; 2411; 2412.

[57] Cf., e.g., canons 2315; 2321; 2322, § 1; 2350, § 2; 2354, § 2.

[58] Cf., e.g., canons 2355; 2405; 2406, § 2.

homine derived penalty can not be indeterminate, but, as he himself admits, the nature of it can be determined at the moment the penalty is inflicted.[59] The opinion which is contrary to that of Coronata, and which is upheld by Salucci,[60] may not be disregarded when there is question of an *ab homine* derived penalty which is indeterminate and which the superior threatens to inflict upon the transgression of a law or precept.

2. *Latae Sententiae* Determined Censures

Any specifically determined censure which is attached to a law or precept in such a manner that it is incurred *ipso facto* by the commission of the delict is to be considered as a *latae sententiae* censure.[61] The term "precept" of canon 2217, § 1, 2° is used generically and therefore includes both general and particular precepts.[62] Cappello, on the contrary, limits the term "precept" of canon 2217, § 1, 2° to signify only a general precept.[63] Since the Code does not distinguish, such a limitation could hardly be the correct interpretation.[64] In his work on public ecclesiastical law Cappello omits mentioning that a general precept is meant by the term "precept," and includes only penalties which are at-

[59] *Ibid.*, p. 76, note 4. Coronata states (*loc. cit.*): ". . . poena ab homine indeterminata repugnare videtur. Cfr. tamen Lega, *loc. cit.*, 78 pag. 105 ubi casus fit poenae ab homine seu per praeceptum peculiare datae, quae tamen indeterminato modo fit, e.g., si Superior dicat: Qui hoc fecerit punietur poena congrua. In hoc casu habetur poena ab homine indeterminata et ferendae sententiae. Attamen ut etiam haec poena revera applicetur delinquenti determinari debere patet." Cf. Lega, *De Delictis et Poenis*, p. 105.

[60] *Diritto Penale*, I, 72. Salucci (*loc. cit.*) admits the existence of indeterminate *ab homine* derived penalties.

[61] Canon 2217, § 1, 2°.

[62] Coronata, *ibid.*, p. 77; Blat, *De Delictis et Poenis*, p. 50. Blat (*loc. cit.*) argues from the legislation of canon 2195 which states that, unless the contrary appears from the circumstances, what is said about offenses is to be applied also to violations of a precept to which a penal sanction is attached. However, Blat (*ibid.*, p. 101) inconsistently interprets the term "*praecepto*" of canon 2245, § 4, to signify only a general precept.

[63] *De Censuris*, n. 4.

[64] Cf. *infra*, p. 90.

tached to general precepts under the definition of penalties determined *a iure.*[65]

The precise concept of a general precept is disputed among authors. A general precept is one which according to common agreement is imposed upon the entire community and not simply upon any single individuals. This may be done in two possible ways, namely, a general precept may be imposed *de facto* upon all the members of the community, but only inasmuch as they are individuals, or a general precept may be imposed directly upon the community as such. In the first instance the precept under all external appearances seems to be numerically one, since it is imposed with one act, but in reality it is multiple, since it is imposed not upon the community as a community, but upon all the individual members of the community for their private good. Some authors maintain that only this kind of precept falls under the species of general precepts.[66] In the second instance the general precept is imposed upon the community as such for the common good of the community.[67] This kind of general precept according to Michiels is essentially a law; a precept exists only when an essential condition is lacking which is required to constitute a law.[68]

An essential condition for the enactment of a law is said to be lacking, for instance, when precepts are imposed by superiors who possess only dominative power, or when they are imposed by a superior who has legislative power but upon an imperfect community, or when they are imposed even upon a perfect community but for a transitory duration, or to provide for some necessity which is of itself temporary. However, for the essential constitution of a true law it is not necessary that the law be established *in perpetuum,* for a law essentially requires only that

---

[65] *Summa Iuris Publici Ecclesiastici ad Normam Codicis Iuris Canonici et Recentiorum S. Sedis Documentorum Concinnata* (4. ed., Romae: Apud Aedes Universitatis Gregorianae, 1936), nn. 94, 96.

[66] Cf. Michiels, *Normae Generales,* I, 520.

[67] Cf. Cicognani, *Ius Canonicum,* II, 151; Coronata, *Institutiones Iuris Canonici,* I, nn. 32, 33; Maroto, *Institutiones Iuris Canonici ad Normam Novi Codicis* (2 vols., Matriti, 1919), I, nn. 263, 268.

[68] Cf. Michiels, *loc. cit.*

stability which precludes it from being a mere transitory or temporary act.[69]

The Code in canons 24, 2217, § 1 and 2245, § 4, foregoes solving the difficulty of interpretation so as to remove all doubt, since in these canons the term "precept" is used without further specification and nowhere in the Code is there found a definition of a general precept. The possibility of either solution therefore remains; but the attempt to limit the term *"praecepto"* as employed in canon 2217, § 1, 2°, so as to signify only a general precept seems rather weak.

In reference to the reservation of *latae sententiae* incurred censures the Code states that a *latae sententiae* censure is not reserved unless this is explicitly stated in the law or precept.[70] Here too the disputed question whether the term "precept" as employed in canon 2217, § 1, 2° and 2245, § 4 is to be limited to signify a general or common precept, or is to be extended to signify all precepts, including particular precepts, arises. If it includes the latter, then a *latae sententiae* determined censure which is attached to a particular precept is not tacitly reserved and to be reserved requires express mention of its reservation. The question will be treated specifically in the following chapter.

3. *Ferendae Sententiae* Determined Censures

In general a *ferendae sententiae* determined penalty is one which in the law or the precept to which it is attached is expressed in such a manner that, once the delict is committed, the penalty has to be inflicted by a judge through a judicial trial, or by a superior outside of a judicial trial. In the meantime the delinquent is not bound to observe the penalty, for it becomes binding only after it has been imposed.[71] In case of doubt whether the penalty is of a

[69] Michiels, *ibid.,* p. 520, note 4.

[70] Canon 2245, § 4. This canon rejects the possibility of any tacit reservation being attached, either by the law or through a precept, to a *latae sententiae* determined censure, which possibility was upheld by D'Annibale before the Code. Cf. D'Annibale, *Summula Theologiae Moralis,* I, p. 345, note 1.

[71] Cf. canon 2217, § 1, 2° . . . (Poena dicitur:) *ferendae sententiae,* si a iudice vel Superiore infligi debeat. . . .

Cf. also, Blat, *De Delictis et Poenis,* p. 50; *Beste, Introductio in Codicem,* p. 889; Ayrinhac, *Penal Legislation,* p. 28.

latae sententiae or a *ferendae sententiae* character the presumption of the law is that the penalty is of the latter kind,[72] since *latae sententiae* penalties are considered more odious in law,[73] and since *ferendae sententiae* penalties are not as easily contracted for the reason that a previous intervention of the judge or the superior is necessary.[74] Since in practice a *ferendae sententiae* applied censure is equivalent to an *ab homine* inflicted censure,[75] the rules governing the reservation of these *ferendae sententiae* applied censures are the same as those governing *ab homine* inflicted censures. These rules will be delineated in section 5 of the present chapter.

4. *A Iure* Derived Censures

The theoretical extension of *a iure* determined penalties depends upon the solution of the question which deals with the matter of precepts in relation to penalties. According to the opinion which contends that a general precept imposed upon a community as a community, and not upon all the members of the community inasmuch as they are individuals, is essentially a law, these same general precepts would be included under the phrase *"in ipsa lege"* of canon 2217, § 1, 3°.[76] According to the opinion which proposes that these general precepts are not essentially laws, the phrase *"in ipsa lege"* does not leave room for the inclusion of these general precepts. Though these authors do not regard a general precept as the equivalent of a law, yet they apply in relation to such a precept the same principle of interpretation as the canon (2217, § 1, 3°) applies in relation to a law which enacts a penal sanction.[77] These authors state that an *a iure* de-

[72] Canon 2217, § 2.

[73] Cappello, *De Censuris*, n. 6; Coronata, *Institutiones Iuris Canonici*, IV, 78; Chelodi, *Ius Poenale*, n. 19.

[74] Beste, *Introductio in Codicem*, p. 889.

[75] Canon 2217, § 1, 3° . . . quare poena ferendae sententiae, legi addita, ante sententiam condemnatoriam est *a iure tantum*, postea *a iure* simul et *ab homine*, sed consideratur tamquam *ab homine*.

[76] Cf. *supra*, p. ??.

[77] Cappello, *De Censuris*, n. 4; Ayrinhac, *Penal Legislation*, p. 64; Beste, *Introductio in Codicem*, p. 889; Vermeersch-Creusen, *Epitome*, III, n. 406.

termined penalty includes not only those penalties which are determined in the law itself but also those penalties which are attached to a general precept. Practically then, both opinions include these general penal precepts under the category of *a iure* determined penalties. Theoretically, the first opinion sees no need of including any species of penal precepts under the category of *a iure* determined penalties.

A iure determined reserved censures are reserved either to the Holy See or to the ordinary.[78]

The words *"Apostolicae Sedi"* of canon 2245, §§ 2, 3, refer not only to the Roman Pontiff but also to the Sacred Congregations and the Roman Tribunals.[79]

The censures which are reserved to the Holy See are reserved either *simpliciter,* or *speciali modo* according to the kind of faculties required for their absolution.[80]

The term "ordinary" is used quite generally, and according to canon 198, § 1, includes the major superiors of clerical exempt religious institutions.[81]

---

[78] Canon 2245, § 2 . . . ex censuris vero *a iure* reservatis aliae sunt reservatae *Ordinario,* aliae *Apostolicae Sedi.*

Cf. canons 2318, § 2; 2330; 2339; 2347, 3°; 2352; 2368, § 2 which furnish examples of *a iure* determined censures (excommunications) which are not reserved.

[79] Canon 7.—Nomine Sedis Apostolicae vel Sanctae Sedis in hoc Codice veniunt non solum Romanus Pontifex, sed etiam, nisi ex rei natura vel sermonis contextu aliud appareat, Congregationes, Tribunalia, Officia, per quae idem Romanus Pontifex negotia Ecclesiae universae expedire solet.

Cf. also Blat, *De Delictis et Poenis,* p. 101. Coronata (*Institutiones Iuris Canonici,* IV, 162) invariably refers to the censures as reserved to the Roman Pontiff.

[80] Canon 2253.—Extra mortis periculum possunt absolvere: 3° . . . a reservata *Sedi Apostolicae,* haec aliive qui absolvendi potestatem ab ea impetraverint sive generalem, si censura *simpliciter reservata* sit, sive specialem, si *reservata speciali modo,* sive denique specialissimam, si *reservata specialissimo modo,* salvo praescripto can. 2254.

Cf. also Blat, *loc. cit.;* Coronata, *loc. cit.;* Beste, *ibid.,* p. 903; Vermeersch-Creusen, *Epitome,* III, n. 442.

[81] Canon 2253.—Extra mortis periculum possunt absolvere:

3°: A *censura a iure reservata,* ille qui censuram constituit vel cui reservata est, eorumque successores aut competentes Superiores aut delegati.

In the external forum only the major superior of clerical exempt institutions has jurisdiction over his subjects; the ordinary of the place can absolve the exempt religious only in the internal sacramental forum from censures incurred by the same religious and reserved to the religious ordinary. When there is question of an *ab homine* inflicted censure the local ordinary cannot absolve the religious subject in either forum.[82]

In the comparison of *latae sententiae* with *a iure* determined penalties it seems in one respect that *latae sententiae* determined penalties have a wider extension than *a iure* determined penalties, while in another respect it seems that *a iure* determined penalties have a wider extension. *Latae sententiae* determined penalties comprehend not only those penalties which are attached to a law, but also those penalties which are attached to a precept, and in this latter respect have a wider extension than *a iure* determined penalties which comprehend only those penalties which are attached to a law.[83] On the other hand, *a iure* determined penalties include not only *latae sententiae* determined penalties but also those which are of a *ferendae sententiae* character, while *latae sententiae* determined penalties are contraposed to *ferendae sententiae* determined penalties.[84]

5. *Ab Homine* Derived Censures

An *ab homine* contracted penalty is one which is inflicted either by way of a particular precept or by means of a condemnatory judicial sentence, even though the penalty is fixed by law. While *ferendae sententiae* penalty which is attached to a law is an *a iure* derived penalty before a condemnatory sentence is issued,

---

Quare a censura reservata *Episcopo* vel *Ordinario,* quilibet Ordinarius absolvere potest suos subditos, loci vero Ordinarius etiam peregrinos. . . .

Cf. Blat, *De Delictis et Poenis,* p. 101; Coronata, *Institutiones Iuris Canonici,* IV, 162; Beste, *Introductio in Codicem,* p. 902. Vermeersch-Creusen assert that the term "*a iure*" in canon 2253, 3°, should be understood to signify *a iure communi.* Cf. Vermeersch-Creusen, *Epitome,* III, 442. Canon 2253, 3°, as quoted in this footnote, does not confirm the interpretation of Vermeersch-Creusen.

[82] Cf. canons 873, § 1; 874; 519; 2253, 2°, 3°. Cf. also Beste, *loc. cit.;* Vermeersch-Creusen, *loc. cit.*

[83] Compare 2° and 3° of canon 2217, § 1.

[84] Compare 2° and 3° of canon 2217,§ 1.

yet it becomes after a condemnatory sentence a penalty which derives both *a iure* and *ab homine.* Once a penalty falls within this latter category, it will be treated juridically as an *ab homine* incurred penalty.[85]

All *ab homine* derived censures are reserved to the one who either inflicted the censure or passed sentence, or to his competent superior, successor or delegate.[86] The fact that all *ab homine* derived censures are strictly reserved can be gathered from parallel canons. No distinction is made between reserved and non-reserved *ab homine* derived censures. The temporary leaving of one's domicile or quasi-domicile does not suspend the reservation of *ab homine* inflicted censures. The Code states in canon 2247, § 2: ". . . Censura vero ab homine est ubique locorum reservata ita ut censuratus nullibi absolvi sine debitis facultatibus possit." The changing of one's domicile or quasi-domicile does not affect the reservation of these censures.

> Canon 2253.—Extra mortis periculum possunt absolvere:
> 2° a censure *ab homine* ille, cui censura reservata est ad normam can. 2245, § 2; ipse autem potest absolutionem concedere, etiamsi reus alio domicilium vel quasi-domicilium transtulerit. . . .

In some instances *ab homine* censures are considered as of equal import with censures reserved *specialissimo modo* to the Holy See, namely, in reference to the efficacy of the absolution which has been granted for them.[87] There can be no doubt, therefore, that all *ab homine* inflicted censures without exception are reserved.

---

[85] Canon 2217, § 1, 3°.

[86] Canon 2245, § 2.

[87] Canon 2247, § 3. Si confessarius, ignorans reservationem, poenitentem a censura ac peccato absolvat, absolutio censurae valet, dummodo ne sit censura ab homine aut censura specialissimo modo Sedi Apostolicae reservata.

Canon 2252.—Qui in periculo mortis constituti, a sacerdote, specialis facultatis experte, receperunt absolutionem ab aliqua censura ab homine vel a censura specialissimo modo Sedi Apostolicae reservata, tenentur, postquam convaluerint, obligatione recurrendi, sub poena reincidentiae, ad illum qui censuram tulit, si agatur de censura ab homine; ad S. Poenitentiariam vel ad Episcopum aliumve facultate praeditum, ad normam can. 2254, § 1, si de censura a iure; eorumque mandatis parendi.

The dissenting opinion of Sole[88] and of Salucci[89] can not be considered as probable.

The assertion of Vermeersch-Creusen that in the old law all *ab homine* derived censures were considered reserved is too general an assertion,[90] for many canonists before the time of Wernz (1842-1914) considered all censures which were incurred through a general precept as being also incurred *ab homine,* but as being not reserved, unless explicit mention of the reservation was made.[91] Lega solved the difficulty by concluding that there existed a *dubium iuris* concerning the question whether these censures were to be considered as deriving *ab homine* and therefore as being reserved, or whether they were to be considered *quasi a iure.*[92] It is however correct to assert that according to the general opinion those *ab homine* derived censures which were inflicted either through a condemnatory sentence or through a particular precept were reserved according to the old law.[93]

A censure which is determined *a iure* (determined by the common law) and is at the same time a *ferendae sententiae* censure after its infliction by means of a condemnatory sentence is reserved to the one who inflicted the censure, and not to the one who constituted the censure or merely applied the censure as a judge.[94] This legislation is in perfect harmony with the teaching

---

[88] *De Delictis et Poenis,* n. 173, 2°.

[89] *Diritto Penale,* I, 199, 200, in nota.

[90] *Epitome,* III, n. 442.

[91] Cf. *supra,* p. ??; cf. also Gury-Ballerini, *Compendium Theologiae Moralis,* II, n. 745; Noldin, *De Poenis Ecclesiasticis* (3. and 4. ed., Oeniponte: Pustet, 1904), n. 28; Lehmkuhl, *Theologia Moralis,* II, 863; Maupied, *Juris Canonici Universi per Faciliorem Methodum ad Veram Praxim Sincere Redacti Compendium* (2 vols., Lutetiae: Parisiis, 1863),. II, p. 1047, 7.

[92] *De Poenis et Delictis,* p. 196.

[93] Cf. Gury-Ballerini, *ibid.,* n. 763; Noldin, *loc. cit.;* Lehmkuhl, *loc. cit.;* Craisson, *Manuale Totius Juris Canonici,* IV, n. 6442; D'Annibale, *Summula Theologiae Moralis,* I, n. 345; St. Alphonsus, *Theologia Moralis,* lib. VII, n. 72; Bucceroni, *Institutiones Theologiae Moralis,* II, n. 1101; Reiffenstuel, *Jus Canonicum Universum,* lib. V, tit. 39, n. 242; Schmalzgrueber, *Jus Ecclesiasticum Universum,* lib. V, tit. 39, nn. 85-88.

[94] Canons 2245, § 2; 2253, 2°; cf. also Ayrinhac, *Penal Legislation,* pp. 28, 63; Woywod, *A Practical Commentary,* II, n. 2086.

of the pre-Code authors.[95] Before the Code Lega treated at length concerning this question. He stated:

> Censurae *fer. sent.* seu quae expostulant sententiam *condemnatoriam specialem a iudice* edendam, sunt reservatae, quoad absolutionem, iudici condemnanti aut iudici appellationis adeo ut Ordinarius huic negotio alienus, absolvere censuram non valeat *ne intercipiatur ordo iurisdictionum.* Quare si postquam sententia condemnationis pertransierit *in rem iudicatam,* ipse censuratus mutet domicilium seu fiat subditus alterius Episcopi, quamvis haec poena sit a iure, eamdem absolvere iste non potest, sed absolvit qui condemnavit nisi expresse absolutio sit *reservata* ipsi legis seu *poenae* latori, quod praecipi non solet.[96]

When there is question of inflicting a censure by means of a condemnatory sentence, the Code demands that the rules for a judicial trial be followed.[97] After a censure is inflicted by means of a condemnatory sentence no appeal can suspend the effects of the sentence.[98] The reservation of a censure to the one who inflicted the penalty by a judicial condemnatory sentence does not apply to those judges who possess a judicial power only.[99]

---

[95] Cf. Lega, *De Delictis et Poenis,* p. 176; Wernz, *Jus Decretalium,* VI, n. 146, and VI, p. 154, note 16.

[96] *De Delictis et Poenis, loc. cit.*

[97] Canon 2225.—Si poena declaretur vel infligatur per sententiam iudicialem, serventur canonum praescripta circa sententiae iudicialis pronuntiationem....

Canon 1959.—In reliquis serventur regulae in Sectione Prima huius Libri traditae et in inflictione poenarum sanctiones in Libro Quinto statutae.

[98] Canon 2243.—Censurae inflictae per sententiam iudicialem, statim ac latae fuerint, executionem secumferunt, nec ab eis datur appellatio, nisi in devolutivo. . . .

Canon 2248 legislates that once a censure has been incurred, it can cease for the penitent only when he has obtained absolution from it.

[99] Canon 2220, § 1 . . . qui (pollent potestate) iudiciali tantum, possunt solummodo poenas, legitime statutas, ad normam iuris applicare.

Canon 2236, § 3. Iudex qui ex officio applicat poenam a Superiore constitutam, eam semel applicatam remittere nequit.

CHAPTER V

LATAE SENTENTIAE Censures Attached to Particular Precepts

The term "*preceptum*" is derived etymologically from the Latin, *prae*, before, and *capio*, take, that is, to take or seize beforehand. Correspondingly it signifies a command made in advance. Juridically a precept is defined: "jussum rationabile a competente Superiore singulis datum."[1] A precept, therefore, is an order or direction, emanating from the competent authority, to individuals, and is not a mere exhortation, a counsel, an instruction, or an admonition.[2]

It is not necessary to solve the question whether the term "competent superior" includes only those who have external jurisdiction or at least some kind of coercive power, for the precepts which are about to be discussed are those to which a *latae sententiae* determined censure is attached. Such precepts automatically exclude religious superiors who have only dominative power over their subjects, and rectors of seminaries and superiors of colleges and pastors.

Particular precepts are imposed upon subjects inasmuch as they are individuals; the purpose of the precept may concern either the private spiritual good of the individual person, or the external disciplinary government of the community. A clear distinction must be drawn between the efficacy of a particular precept in relation to judicial and extra-judicial procedure. A particular precept which is not imposed according to the norms of canon 24[3] cannot be enforced by judicial process, but it is not correct to

---

[1] Cf. canon 24: "*Praecepta, singulis data,* eos quibus dantur, ubique urgent. . . ." Cf. also Michiels, *Normae Generales,* I, 507; Cicognani, *Canon Law* (2. revised ed., authorized English version, translated by J. M. O'Hara and F. Brennan, Philadelphia: Dolphin Press, 1935), p. 634.

[2] Cf. Michiels, *ibid.,* p. 508; Cicognani, *loc. cit.*

[3] Canon 24.—Praecepta, singulis data, . . . iudicialiter urgeri nequent . . . nisi per legitimum documentum aut coram duobus testibus imposita fuerint.

conclude therefrom that precepts which are given privately to individuals bind them in the internal forum only, for such precepts belong to the external extrajudicial forum.[4] If the infliction of certain penalties requires a judicial process then the observance of the stipulations of canon 24 is prerequired if the violation of the precept is to be punished judicially. Precepts given privately to individuals can not become a basis for the judicial infliction of penalties. For example, if a religious superior imposed a precept upon a subject even under the vow of obedience but privately, he would be unable to use the transgression in order to proceed judicially in the dismissal of the religious.[5]

The Code states that censures may be inflicted without judicial process,[6] but the Code specifies that in the declaration or infliction of a *latae* or *ferendae sententiae* determined penalty through a particular precept certain formalities are ordinarily required.[7] It is understood that if a *latae sententiae* determined censure which is attached to a particular precept is to be incurred actually, the crime must be an act which is external, grave, consummated or complete, and combined with contumacy.[8] A person is said to be contumacious if he transgresses the precept to which the *latae sententiae* determined censure is attached.[9]

The infliction or declaration of penalties, therefore, without judicial process is not to be understood to mean that the infliction or declaration of the penalty can be done in an arbitrary manner; this must be done in accord with the manner of procedure determined by the Code for the different instances.[10] The inflic-

---

[4] Michiels, *ibid.*, p. 519; Cicognani, *ibid.*, p. 638.

[5] Cf. canons 659-663.

[6] Canon 1933, § 4 . . . excommunicatio, suspensio, interdictum, dummodo delictum certum sit, infligi possunt etiam per modum praecepti extra iudicium.

[7] Canon 2225 . . . si vero poena latae vel ferendae sententiae inflicta sit ad modum praecepti particularis, scripto aut coram duobus testibus ordinarie declaretur vel irrogetur, indicatis poenae causis. . . .

[8] Canon 2242, § 1.

[9] Canon 2242, § 2.

[10] Cf. Noval, "De ratione Corrigendi ac Puniendi sive in Judicio sive extra Jure Codicis Juris Canonici"—*Jus Pont.*, III (1923), 205.

tion of penalties by means of a particular precept is one of these determined procedures.[11]

Noval distinguishes between the first procedure, namely, the one to be observed in inflicting a *ferendae sententiae* penalty which is attached to a particular precept, and the second or declaratory manner of procedure, namely, the one to be observed in declaring a *latae sententiae* incurred penalty which is attached to a particular precept.[12] When there is no penalty attached to a law the Code permits legitimate superiors without previous threat of penalty to punish a transgression with some just penalty, if the scandal given or the special gravity of the violation demands it. This is the third manner of proceeding.[13] Further, when the ordinary cannot without grave inconvenience proceed against his subject in the ordinary course of law, he may punish his clerical subjects with suspension from office *ex informata conscientia,* and this suspension may be either partial or total.[14] Finally, if the ordinary undertakes to punish clerics who are violating the law of residence or who are living in concubinage, or a pastor who is neglecting to fulfill his pastoral duties, he is obliged to follow respectively one of the manners of procedure which is specified in canons 2168-2185.

A difficult and disputed problem arises in determining the reservation or non-reservation of those censures which are attached to particular precepts and are incurred *ipso facto* through a violation of these precepts. This difficulty arises from the comparing of paragraph 2 with paragraph 4 in canon 2245. In the second paragraph[15] this canon states that a censure which derives *ab homine* is reserved to the one who inflicted it or pro-

---

[11] Cf. canons 1933, § 4; 2225. For other ways of inflicting penalties cf. canons 2222, § 1; 2168-2185; 2186-2194.

[12] *Art. cit.,* pp. 205, 206. For the first manner of procedure, cf. canons 1933, § 4, 2225; 2233, § 2; 2242, §§ 2, 3. For the second manner of procedure, cf. canon 2225.

[13] Cf. canon 2222, § 1.

[14] Cf. canons 2186-2194.

[15] Canon 2245, § 2. Censura *ab homine* est reservata ei qui censuram inflixit aut sententiam tulit, eiusve Superiori competenti, vel successori aut delegato; ex censuris vero *a iure* reservatis aliae sunt reservatae *Ordinario,* aliae *Apostolicae Sedi.*

nounced a judicial sentence, or to his competent Superior, successor, or delegate; in the fourth paragraph[16] this canon states that a *latae sententiae* contracted censure is not reserved unless the reservation be clearly stated in the law or the precept. *Ab homine* inflicted censures, therefore, are reserved, while *latae sententiae* censures are not reserved unless the contrary be stated. Now the question arises whether a *latae sententiae* contracted censure which is attached to a particular precept is to be considered 1) as deriving solely *ab homine* and therefore reserved; 2) as a *latae sententiae* censure which at the same time derives *ab homine* but is not reserved; or 3) as a *latae sententiae* censure not deriving *ab homine* and therefore not reserved. Canonists who maintain the last mentioned interpretation assert that such a censure is *"tamquam a iure"*[17] or *"per praeceptum ad instar legis."*[18] The opinion of the authors will be treated according to the order of the evolution and the development of the dispute.

There are many authors who find no difficulty whatsoever in the treatment of paragraphs 2 and 4 of canon 2245 and assume that the reservation of censures in particular precepts to which a *latae sententiae* derived censure has been attached is not dubious. They at least suppose that all these *latae sententiae* contracted censures attached to particular precepts are to be considered as *ab homine* and, as a consequence, necessarily reserved. Among these authors are found Cerato,[19] Cippollini,[20] Crnica,[21] Ferreres (1861-1936),[22]

---

[16] Canon 2245, § 4. Censura latae sententiae non est reservata, nisi in lege vel praecepto id expresse dicatur; et in dubio sive iuris sive facti reservatio non urget.

[17] Michiels, "De reservatione censurae latae sententiae praecepto peculiari adnexae"—*ETL,* IV (1927), 192.

[18] Roberti, "An censura latae sententiae per praeceptum constituta sit reservata?"—*Apollinaris* (Romae, 1928-), VI (1933), 342.

[19] *Censurae Vigentes Ipso Facto a Codice Iuris Canonici Excerptae* (2. ed., Patavii: Typis Seminarii, 1921), n. 15, 1°-6°.

[20] *De Censuris Latae Sententiae iuxta Codicem Iuris Canonici,* nn. 10, 2°; 12, 4°; 42, c).

[21] *Modificationes in Tractatu de Censuris per Codicem Iuris Canonici Introductae* (S. Mauritii Agaunensis: Typis op. S. Augustini, 1919), pp. 9, 50.

[22] *Institutiones Canonicae* (2. ed., 2 vols., Barcinone: Subirana, 1920), II, nn. 998, 999.

Genicot-Salsmans[23] and Prümmer (1866-1931).[24] Other authors who also do not consider the issue doubtful expressly affirm that all *latae sententiae* contracted censures which are attached to particular precepts are to be considered as deriving *ab homine* and as being reserved.[25]

Sole is the first author after the Code who holds an opinion contrary to the common opinion concerning the *latae sententiae* contracted censures which are attached to particular precepts.[26] According to him not all censures which are derived *ab homine* are reserved, since he considers the *latae sententiae* contracted censures which are attached to particular precepts as being *ab homine* and at the same time not reserved, unless the contrary is expressly stated.[27] After Sole, this solution was upheld by the *Monitore Ecclesiastico*[28] and also by Salucci.[29] Coronata does not consider this opinion improbable and therefore maintains that the opinion can be followed in practice until the Holy See should authentically decide otherwise.[30] The second part of canon 2245, § 4, and also canon 2246, § 2, are employed by Coronata to solve the apparent contradiction in the second paragraph and the first part of the fourth paragraph of canon 2245.[31]

---

[23] *Institutiones Theologiae Moralis,* II, 564.

[24] *Manuale Iuris Canonici in Usum Scholarum* (3. ed., Friburgi Brisgoviae, 1922), p. 637, quaest. 568.

[25] E.g., Blat (*De Delictis et Poenis,* n. 34, 3°): "*ab homine* imponitur, *si feratur per modum praecepti* peculiaris uni vel pluribus dati, cui adnexa sit per comminationem aut inflictionem, . . ."; (*ibid.,* n. 69): "*Censura* quaelibet *ab homine, . . . est reservata* vi huius praescripti a) *ei qui censuram* illam singularem *inflixit* per modum praecepti peculiaris, . . ."; Chelodi (*Ius Poenale et Ordo Procedendi in Iudiciis Criminalibus iuxta Codicem Iuris Canonici,* n. 19, 3): "*Ab homine tantum* est poena addita praecepto peculiari." (*ibid.,* n. 33, a): "Omnes censurae *ab homine* sunt reservatae et quidem illi qui aut praeceptum imposuit aut sententiam dixit."

[26] Sole (*De Delictis et Poenis,* n. 173, 2°): "*Censura l. s., sive sit a iure, sive ab homine per praeceptum, nisi expresse dicatur in lege vel praecepto, non est reservata,* can. 2245, § 4."

[27] *De Delictis et Poenis, loc. cit.*

[28] "Il Codice di Diritto Canonico-Riasunto e Dilucidazioni"—*Il Monitore Ecclesiastico* (Romae, 1876-), Serie IV, Vol. IV (1922), 147.

[29] *Diritto Penale,* I, 199, 200, in nota.

[30] *Institutiones Iuris Canonici,* IV, 163, ad notam 2.

[31] *Ibid.,* 163: "Cum in dubio sive iuris sive facti reservatio non urget et cum generatim reservatio sit odiosa et strictam recipere debeat interpretationem et cum revera in hoc casu agi videatur de dubio iuris seu de

Creusen,[82] examining the doubt caused by paragraphs 2 and 4 of can. 2245, in 1924 argued that the principle which is proposed in canon 6, 4°, concerning the presumed conformity with the old law affects the entire Code, and that all other rules, e.g., canons 23, 2219, 2245, etc., are subordinate. The old law, he concludes, can not be changed concerning canon 2245.

However, in 1928 he modified his view by admitting at least the existence of a *dubium iuris,*[83] and admonished superiors to be clear in the wording of censures inflicted by particular precepts.[84] More specifically, he asserted that the Code in defining an *ab homine* inflicted punishment together with some pre-Code authors, e.g., Lega,[85] and Wernz,[86] prefers to include the words *"per modum praecepti peculiaris,"* as referring to all particular precepts whether they are of a *latae* or *ferendae sententiae* character.[87] The argument proceeds: these same pre-Code authors considered a censure inflicted by a general precept as not reserved, unless the reservation was expressly stated, and therefore if the words *"lege vel praecepto"* of canon 2245, § 4, are understood to designate both a general law or a particular statute or also a general precept, then there is harmony not only among the texts but also with the old law and the doctrine of those whom the Legislator without doubt has followed.[88]

The following remarks may be made in reference to Creusen's view. The limiting of the term *"praecepto"* in canon 2245, § 4, to signify only a general precept seems to do violence to the text,

---

lege dubia, dicemus censuram quamlibet latae sententiae sive ab homine sive a iure non reservari nisi in lege vel praecepto sive generali sive particulari expresse dicatur."

[82] "De Reservatione Censurae Praecepto Latae"—*Jus Pont.,* IV (1924), 26-29.

[83] "La reserve des censures 'ab homine,'"—*Nouvelle Revue Théologique* (Parisiis, 1869-), LV (1928), 444. (Henceforth abbreviated as *NRT.*)

[84] *Art. cit.,* p. 445.

[85] Cf. *supra,* p. 71.

[86] Cf. *supra,* pp. 69-70.

[87] Can. 2217, § 1, 3° . . . *ab homine,* si feratur per modum praecepti peculiaris vel. . . .

[88] Creusen, "De Reservatione Censurae Praecepto Latae"—*Jus Pont.* IV (1924), 28-29. Cf. also Ayrinhac, *Penal Legislation* (New York: Benziger, 1936), p. 64.

for the normal method of interpretation suggests that it refers to both the general and the particular precept, or at least to the particular precept.[39] The interpretation of the old law is to be followed if it is not contrary to the Code itself,[40] or if harmony among the texts cannot otherwise be established. A careful and more complete study of the old law is required to determine whether the old law concerning *latae sententiae* contracted censures which are attached to particular precepts was clear. This Michiels undertakes to do.[41] But before the consideration of Michiels' arguments Cappello's opinion, which was also adopted by DeMeester,[42] will be treated.

Cappello, as Creusen does, limits the term *"praecepto"* in canon 2245, § 4, to a general precept,[43] and asserts that all the *latae sententiae* contracted censures in the above mentioned section of canon 2245 are either *a iure* or imposed *per modum censurarum a iure*.[44] A more thorough consideration of four arguments which he proposes to refute Sole's opinion (namely, that *latae sententiae* determined censures which are attached to particular precepts are of an *ab homine* character, but are not reserved, unless the opposite is stated) will help to evaluate Cappello's view

[39] Cf. Michiels, "De reservatione censurae 1. s. praecepto peculiari adnexae"—*ETL*, IV (1927), 185; Roberti, "An censura latae sententiae per praeceptum constituta sit reservata?"—*Apollinaris*, VI (1933), 344 and 346; Salucci, *Diritto Penale*, I, 199, in nota; Rainer, *Suspension of Clerics*, The Catholic University of America Canon Law Studies, n. 111 (Washington, D. C.: The Catholic University of America, 1937), p. 9; Moriarty, *The Extraordinary Absolution from Censures*, The Catholic University of America Canon Law Studies, n. 113 (Washington, D. C.: The Catholic University of America, 1938), p. 98.

[40] Canon 6.

[41] "De reservatione censurae latae sententiae praecepto peculiari adnexae" —*ETL*, IV (1927), 613-619.

[42] *Canonici et Juris Canonico-Civilis Compendium* (nova ed., 3 vols. in 4, Brugis: Desclée, 1921-1928), n. 1736, 2°. Vermeersch-Creusen (*Epitome*, III, nn. 442, 443), prefer Cappello's view to that of Sole's, but in accepting Cappello's opinion, they reject Cappello's statement that a censure attached to a particular precept is reserved only after the declaratory sentence.

[43] *De Censuris*, n. 68.

[44] *Loc. cit.* According to Cappello the censures inflicted *per modum censurarum a iure* are those which the superior imposes upon the whole community by a general precept.

regarding the question. His first argument is: canon 2245, § 2, clearly distinguishes between an *ab homine* derived censure inflicted by means of a judicial sentence and a censure inflicted by means of a precept, and both are reserved. The first member of paragraph 2, *"qui censuram inflixit,"* refers to a censure inflicted *ad modum praecepti particularis* either in writing or before two witnesses according to the prescriptions of canon 2225, and the second member, *"sententiam tulit,"* refers to a censure inflicted through a judicial sentence.[45] For the second argument he adduces the statement of canon 2252, which imposes an obligation of recourse upon a person who in danger of death has received from a priest without faculties absolution from any *ab homine* inflicted censure. The penitent is under obligation to make a recourse to him *"qui censuram tulit, si agatur de censura ob homine."* Since the law does not distinguish, he argues, the obligation of recourse exists for every censure which is of an *ab homine* nature, regardless of whether the censure had been imposed (*lata sit*) through a judicial sentence or through a particular precept. According to Cappello, therefore, all *ab homine* derived censures are *reserved* and under *ab homine* derived are included both *ferendae* and *latae sententiae* determined censures which are attached to particular precepts.[46] His third argument is founded in canon 2253, 2°,[47] and differs from the former argu-

[45] Cappello, *op. cit.*, n. 68, 1°. The reservation or non-reservation of particular precepts would thus depend upon the act of declaration, but nowhere does the Code teach that a declaratory sentence has any such effect upon the reservation of *latae sententiae* determined penalties. On the contrary, the Code rather seems to imply the opposite in canons 2223, § 4, and 2232, § 2. Cf. Roberti, "An censura latae sententiae per praeceptum constituta sit reservata?"—*Apollinaris,* VI (1933), 347-348. Cappello (*De Censuris,* n. 76) admits that a declaratory sentence would not affect the reservation or non-reservation of *a iure* derived censures, since an *a iure* derived censure would not become *ab homine* by the declaration.

[46] Cappello, *De Censuris,* 68, 2°. Canon 2252.—Qui in periculo mortis constituti, a sacerdote, specialis facultatis experte, receperunt absolutionem *ab aliqua censura ab homine,* vel . . . tenentur, postquam convaluerint, obligatione recurrendi, sub poena reincidentiae, *ad illum qui censuram tulit, si agatur de censura ab homine;* . . . (Italics not in the original text.)

[47] Canon 2253.—Extra mortis periculum possunt absolvere:

2° A censura *ab homine,* ille, cui censura reservata est ad normam can. 2245, § 2.

Cf. *De Censuris,* n. 68, 3°.

ment in as much as the former dealt with absolutions in danger of death, while the latter deals with absolutions outside the danger of death. For the canon which deals with absolution from *ab homine* inflicted censures outside of the danger of death also does not distinguish between reserved and non-reserved censures which are of an *ab homine* character, but considers as reserved all *ab homine* derived censures without any exception. As his fourth and conclusive argument he brings to light the explicit declaration of canon 2247, § 2, which speaks of a *censura ab homine* without any further qualifications as being reserved everywhere.[48]

In connection with Cappello's arguments the following remarks may be made. From these last three arguments the logical and valid conclusion is: whenever a censure is *ab homine* that censure is reserved. This conclusion can not be denied. The first argument demonstrates that the Code manifestly distinguishes between a censure derived *ab homine* which is inflicted through a condemnatory sentence and one which is inflicted through a precept. The question at issue, however, is whether a *latae sententiae* contracted censure attached to particular precept is to be included under the first member of paragraph 2, *"qui censuram inflixit."*

Michiels, on the contrary, asserts that *latae sententiae* determined censures which are incurred because of the violation of a particular precept are not derived *ab homine,* and therefore not reserved. His main arguments can be summed up as follows:

1. From the text itself of canon 2245, § 4, or from the consideration of the words alone it is evident that general terminology is used in reference to censures which are contracted as *latae sententiae* penalties. To limit the term *"praeceptum"* to a *"praeceptum commune"* appears to do violence to the text, since in the entire Code the term *"praeceptum"* is understood to signify every precept properly so-called or at least a particular precept.[49]

2. According to the norms of correct interpretation, the words

[48] *De Censuris,* n. 68, 4°: "'Censura vero ab homine (sine ulla distinctione) est *ubique locorum reservata,* ita ut censuratus nullibi absolvi sine debitis facultatibus possit.' Haec verba adeo sunt clara et explicita ut certo constet, opinionem, de qua supra, tuto defendi non posse, cum lex ipse eam improbet atque reiiciat."

[49] Michiels, "De reservatione censurae latae sententiae praecepto peculiari adnexae"—*ETL,* IV (1927), 185. Cf. also *supra*, p. 91.

which the legislator uses to determine a certain juridical concept are to be understood to have the same meaning which he has attributed to these same juridical concepts in a preceding canon written precisely in order to determine aptly those juridical concepts. But canon 2217, § 1, 2°, presents the juridical concept of a *latae sententiae* determined penalty and uses the words, "si poena determinata ita sit addita legi vel praecepto . . . ," and thus refers to general and particular precepts alike. Therefore canon 2245, § 4, is to be understood to refer to both general and particular precepts.[50]

3. In canon 2217 *a iure* derived censures are opposed to *ab homine* derived censures, and *latae sententiae* determined censures are opposed to *ferendae sententiae* determined censures, while in canon 2245 the opposition is evidently between *ab homine* derived censures and *latae sententiae* determined censures. In canon 2244 the same opposition takes place between § 2 and § 3. Therefore, *ab homine* and *latae sententiae* determined censures constitute two adequate and exclusive species, which taken together constitute the genus of censures.[51]

4. In the definition of an *ab homine* derived penalty it is evident that the verb *"feratur"* is to be understood univocally of both members. Now since *"feratur"* is understood in the second member to signify an infliction by a special punitive act of the judge or superior, it must also signify an infliction by a special punitive act in reference to *"per modum praecepti peculiaris."* Logically then in canon 2245, § 2, the clause *"qui censuram inflixit,"* which is to be considered parallel to the clause *"feratur per modum*

---

[50] *Ibid.*, pp. 185, 186.

[51] *Ibid.*, p. 188. Roberti ("An censura latae sententiae per praeceptum constituta sit reservata?"—*Apollinaris,* VI [1933,] 343, note [4]) says: "Distinctiones autem non sunt identicae, secus inutiliter ambae proponerentur; nam poena *ferendae* sententiae *ante applicationem* est *a iure.* Ergo latius patet poena *a iure* quam poena *latae sententiae.*" Michiels, however, must have had in mind to set forth a practical division of censures rather than a theoretical division or the manner of considering censures before their infliction. *A iure* determined censures which are of a *ferendae sententiae* character are included under *ab homine* derived censures after application or infliction. Then *latae sententiae* and *ab homine* determined censures constitute an adequate division.

praecepti peculiaris," has the same meaning, namely, an infliction by a special punitive act.[52]

5. The old law upon which authors of the opposing opinion base their arguments did not deal expressly with *latae sententia* contracted censures which are attached to particular precepts, and many authors, as Suarez (1548-1617), Layman (1515-1635), Pirhing (1606-1679), Reiffenstuel (1641-1703), Mansi (1692-1769), Collet (1693-1770), Pauwels (✠ after 1759) and Kober (1821-1897) present the reservation as truly uncertain or seem to favor the non-reservation of these precepts, while others, as Thesaurus (1587-1655) and Berardi (1719-1768) affirm their non-reservation.[53]

The contentions of Michiels will be seen in a clearer light after the answers to three of the proposed objections are considered. The first objection arises from the consideration of canon 2225, in which the phrase *"inflicta sit"* is used in connection with the phrase *"poena latae vel ferendae sententiae."* Michiels answers that this is the only example in which the Code proceeds in this manner and that the term *"inflicta sit"* is equivalent to *"comminata fuerit."*[54] Michiels, supposing but not granting that canon 2225 is opposed to his interpretation, insists that the probatory value of the other arguments is not weakened.[55]

---

[52] *Ibid.*, pp. 190, 191. Cf. also, Rainer, *Suspension of Clerics,* p. 50.

[53] *Ibid.*, pp. 616-618; cf. *supra*, pp. 66-69.

[54] *Ibid.*, p. 191, note 23. If, however, canon 2225 is studied more closely, it appears that the term *"inflicta sit"* is used in a wider sense, namely, "si vero poena *latae* vel *ferendae sententiae* inflicta sit" (meaning the actual incurring in reference to the *latae sententiae* penalty; while in reference to a *ferendae sententiae* penalty it connotes *"comminata fuerit"*). This interpretation seems to be confirmed in the remaining words of the canon: ". . . ordinarie *declaretur*," referring back to the *latae sententiae* incurred penalty, "vel *irrogetur*," referring to the *ferendae sententiae* to be applied penalty. The act of both the declaration of the *latae sententiae* determined censure and the threatened infliction of the *ferendae sententiae* determined censure presupposes a delict, or more specifically the violation of the precept.

[55] Michiels considers canon 2225 as constructed *"infelici modo" (loc. cit.)*. This, however, need not be admitted. Insistence should be placed not upon the use of the verb *"inflicta sit"* itself, but upon the fact that the purpose of canon 2225 is to deal with the declaration and application of penalties in general; while the purpose of canon 2245 is to determine in particular the rules for the reservation of censures. As a consequence the construction of canon 2225 need not be censured.

Moriarty states that the infliction of a *latae sententiae* determined penalty takes place and is established in the precept, and is based on a suspensive condition.[56] He denies that the word "*inflicta*" is to be understood in a double sense, namely, as "*irrogetur*" when referred to *ferendae sententiae* determined penalties, and as either "*comminetur*" or "*declaretur*" when referred to *latae sententiae* determined penalties, for, he asserts, neither the threat nor the declaration of a *latae sententiae* determined penalty is by any means an infliction.[57] The most that can be conceded is that the imposition of a particular precept to which is added a *ferendae sententiae* determined censure can be considered only as an incipient exercise which leads to the actual infliction of the penalty, but in no way can it be considered as an infliction, since as yet there is no violation of the precept.[58] A *latae sententiae* determined censure is strictly speaking incurred.[59] All of Moriarty's submitted examples in which the Code uses the term "inflict" in connection with *latae sententiae* determined censures are such in which the Code includes both *latae* and *ferendae sententiae* determined censures.[60]

Whenever the Code speaks of *latae sententiae* determined censures only, it invariably uses, not the term "inflict," but the term "incur."[61] Whenever the Code speaks of *ferendae sententiae* determined censures only, it invariably uses the term "*inflict.*"[62]

---

[56] *The Extraordinary Absolution from Censures,* p. 102.

[57] *Ibid.,* p. 102, note 40.

[58] Canon 2233, § 1. Nulla poena infligi potest, nisi certo constet delictum commissum fuisse et non esse legitime praescriptum.

Cf. also § 2 of the same canon.

[59] Canon 2242, § 2 . . . ad incurrendam vero censuram latae sententiae sufficit transgressio legis vel praecepti. . . .

Canon 2217, § 1, 2° (Poena dicitur): *Latae sententiae,* si poena determinata ita sit addita legi vel praecepto ut incurratur ipso facto commissi delicti. . . .

[60] Cf. canons 2241, § 2; 2220, § 2; 2236, § 1; 2225.

[61] Cf. footnote n. 59. Cf. also canons 2243, § 2; 2244, § 2.

[62] Cf., e.g., canons 2217, § 1, 2°; 2223, § 2, § 3; 2233, § 1, § 2; 2243, § 1; 1933, § 4; 2244, § 3.

Canon 2244, § 3. Censura *ab homine* multiplicatur, si plura *praecepta* . . . vel plures distinctae partes eiusdem praecepti aut sententiae suam quaeque censuram *infligant.* (Italics not in original text.)

The violation of the precept establishes the basis for declaring a *latae sententiae* incurred censure, and the incurring of the censure itself can only in a wider sense be understood as being *"inflicta"* according to the use of this word in canon 2225; on the other hand, the violation of the precept establishes the basis for inflicting a *ferendae sententiae* determined censure, and the actual infliction only can in the strict sense be understood as connoted by the word *"inflicta."* Since canon 2225 establishes the act of declaration (in reference to *latae sententiae* determined censures) and the act of infliction (in reference to *ferendae sententiae* determined censures), the violation of the precept is necessarily presupposed, and the verbal form *"inflicta sit"* is of inherent necessity to be understood in a wider sense. This conclusion is confirmed by canon 2243, § 1, § 2, where the Code uses the following terminology in reference to censures applied *"per modum praecepti"*:

> Can. 2243, § 1: . . . item a *censuris ad modum praecepti inflictis* datur recursus, sed in devolutivo tantum. (Italics not in the original text.)
>
> Can. 2243, § 2: Appellatio vero vel recursus a sententia iudiciali vel *praecepto comminante censuras etiam latae sententiae nondum contractas,* nec sententiam aut praeceptum nec censuras suspendunt. . . . (Italics not in the original text.)

Paragraph 1 of the cited canon refers strictly to censures which are actually inflicted *per modum praecepti* and which are consequently of a *ferendae sententiae* character. Paragraph 2 of the cited canon refers to non-contracted censures which are strictly threatened *per praeceptum,* and which may be of a *latae* or *ferendae sententiae* character. In the first part of the first paragraph the Code states:

> Canon 2243, § 1: Censurae inflictae per sententiam iudicialem, statim ac latae fuerint, executionem secumferunt. . . .

The term *"inflictae"* here excludes the threat of censure but refers to the actual infliction, since in paragraph two of the same canon the Code deals with the threatening of censures.

Coronata deals at length with the implications of the term *"inflicta sit,"* and asserts:

> Canone 2225 supponitur poenam latae sententiae infligi posse per praeceptum particulare, at ibi non dicitur posse imponi per praeceptum, sed infligi ad modum praecepti; proinde ibi vox *infligi* improprie accipi videtur cum pro declaratione, tum pro vere et proprie dicta inflictione seu poenae applicatione. Et tunc facile intelligitur qua ratione poena latae sententiae ad modum praecepti declarari possit. Declaratio ad modum praecepti poenae latae sententiae a iure latae est declaratio poenae incursae extraiudicialiter facta ad normam c. 2225. Hoc in casu praeceptum seu declaratio ad modum praecepti sententiae declaratoriae aequivalet et . . . consideratur ut poena a iure non ut poena ab homine. . . .[63]

The second objection is: A particular precept is imposed by a definite superior upon an individual. Therefore it has to be considered *ab homine.* In the answer Michiels distinguishes between the precept and the censure; the precept is derived *ab homine* but the censure attached to the precept is not necessarily derived *ab homine. In actu primo* the precept is derived *ab homine,* since it is personally imposed by the superior or judge, but *in actu secundo* the censure can be said to derive *ab homine* only then when it is actually inflicted *ab homine individuo in determinatam personam.*[64]

In response to the third objection, namely, that the quasi-judicial order of procedure is infracted,[65] Michiels states that the

[63] *Institutiones Iuris Canonici,* IV, 77.

[64] Michiels, "De reservatione censurae latae sententiae praecepto peculiari adnexae,"—*ETL,* IV (1927), 193.

[65] This objection is drawn from the teaching of Creusen ("De reservatione censurae praecepto latae"—*Ius Pont.,* IV [1924], 26-29, especially on p. 29) who contends that a superior at the very time when he imposes a precept with a *latae sententiae* censure annexed to it acts as a judge who passes sentence, for the same superior does not at any later time intervene with any pronouncement for the application of the censure when the precept has been violated. Creusen thereupon asks: "Isn't it true, then, even

superior, when he imposes the particular precept, does not institute a judicial pronouncement after the fashion of condemnatory sentence, for he does not then actually inflict the censure, since no censure can be said to be inflicted when it is merely threatened. Nor does the superior intervene judicially after the delictual act has been committed, for the very commission of the delict suffices for the incurring of the threatened censure.[66] And even if one granted that an infraction of the judicial order were present, such an infraction is evidently permitted in canon 2252 with reference to a penitent who is granted absolution when he is in danger of death, or also in the case of a confession which is made with a view to the gaining of the Jubilee Indulgences.[67]

Cocchi, considering the arguments proposed by Michiels, concluded that they are not without foundation and that they contribute largely to the clarification of the doctrine of reservation.[68] He, himself, however, adheres to the opposite opinion which holds that *latae sententiae* censures, when they are incurred in consequence of the violation of a particular precept, are reserved.[69]

According to Kinane, Michiels' view has no probability whatever.[70] First he denies the restriction of the term *"ferre"* of canon 2217, § 1, 3° so as to make it convey the meaning of infliction, or the placing of a special punitive act by the superior.[71]

---

though it be less flagrantly so than in the case wherein a condemnatory sentence has been pronounced that the requisite procedure within the judicial order would be obstructed, if some one other than the same superior, or his successor, etc., absolved from the incurred censure?"

[66] Michiels, *art. cit.*, p. 194.

[67] Cf. Pius XI, const. *"Si unquam alias,"* 15 iul. 1924, I-II—*AAS*, XVI (1924), 310.

[68] "SIC SUBTILITER, DECISIVE ET *eleganter* argumentatur P. GOMMARUS MICHIELS . . . *et non sine fundamento* (ut videtur), *et quidem cum magno incremento* CLARITATIS doctrinae reservationis QUAE deficit in sententia opposita, licet, saltem *auctoritate externa*, multo magis suffragata; huius Auctoris rationes tales sunt ut ipsi videatur licita conclusio nos hic versari, *pro praxi*, in vero casu *dubii iuris*."—*Commentarium in Codicem Iuris Canonici*, VIII, 113.

[69] *Ibid.*, p. 112.

[70] "The Reservation of Censures 'Latae Sententiae' Imposed by a Particular Precept,"—*Irish Ecclesiastical Record* (Dublin, 1864-), XL (1932), 534. (Hereafter abbreviated as *IER*.)

[71] *Ibid.*, pp. 530-532; cf. also Ayrinhac, *Penal Legislation*, p. 64; Beste, *Introductio in Codicem*, p. 903.

In reference to this denial the following facts should be taken into consideration: *"ferre"* considered in itself undoubtedly can be employed in the generic sense, and is not to be restricted to the meaning of actual infliction in relation to *ferendae sententiae* censures only. The terms *"infligere," "ferre,"* are used by the Code itself to signify the imposition of *latae sententiae* determined censures, e.g., in canon 2241, § 2: "Censurae, praesertim latae sententiae, maxime excommunicatio, ne *infligantur,* nisi sobrie et magna cum circumspectione" and in canon 2236, § 1: "Remissio poenae sive per absolutionem, si agatur de censuris, sive per dispensationem, si de poenis vindicativis, concedi tantum potest ab eo qui poenam *tulit,* . . ." The context has to determine the precise manner of the infliction of the penalty. In a few canons it is evident that the Legislator is referring to *ferendae sententiae* penalties only.[72]

Since the meaning of the clause *"qui censuram inflixit"* in canon 2245, § 2 is disputed, it is necessary to recur to other canons which may help to clarify the precise meaning of the term "infligere." Canon 2217, § 1, 3°, considers the case of a censure derived *ab homine* if it is inflicted *per modum praecepti peculiaris,* and the Code, in treating of censures inflicted *per modum praecepti,* refers to *ferendae sententiae* censures which are inflicted by a special punitive act.[73] Moreover, within the definition of *ab homine* derived censures there are contained both the censures inflicted *per modum praecepti peculiaris* and also the censures inflicted *per sententiam iudicialem condemnatoriam, etsi in iure statuta.* These two kinds of censures are considered in parallel fashion, and in canons 1933, § 4, and 2243, § 1, both are treated in a similar manner. This induces one to acknowledge a similarity of nature between censures *ferendae sententiae* inflicted *per modum praecepti,* which censures correspond to the first member of the definition of

[72] E.g., in canon 2233, § 1. Nulla poena infligi potest, nisi certo constet delictum commissum fuisse et non esse legitime praescriptum. . . .

Cf. also canons 2233, § 2; 2224, § 2, § 3; 1933, § 4.

[73] Cf. canon 1933, § 4. Poenitentia, remedium poenale, excommunicatio, suspensio, interdictum, dummodo delictum certum sit, infligi possunt etiam per modum praecepti extra iudicium. . . .

2243, § 1 . . . item a censuris ad modum praecepti inflictis datur recursus, sed in devolutivo tantum.

ab homine derived censures, and censures inflicted *per sententiam iudicialem condemnatoriam* (regardless of whether or not they originate *a iure*), which censures correspond to the second member of the definition.[74] Further, the Code in treating of the multiplication of censures seems to imply that a *latae sententiae* determined censure which is attached to a particular precept is not to be included under *ab homine* derived censures. The Code states that censures derived *ab homine* are multiplied, if each of the several precepts, or several distinct parts of the same precept, *inflict* a censure.[75] This rule holds for all censures derived *ab homine*, unless the opposite can be proved. But a *latae sententiae* determined censure which is attached to a particular precept is multiplied not only, if each of several precepts determines a censure, which is evident in itself, but also if the same offense to which a censure is attached is committed repeatedly in such a manner that the repeated acts constitute several distinct offenses.[76] This manner of multiplication of censures is not applicable to *ab homine* derived censures or to *ferendae sententiae* determined censures.

Further, Kinane, arguing against the view of Michiels that canon 2245, § 4, applies to penalties *per modum praecepti par-*

---

[74] Cf. Roberti, "An censura latae sententiae per praeceptum constituta sit reservata? ". . . sensus verbi 'feratur' ex contextu *(feratur per modum praecepti peculiaris)*, collatis locis parallelis . . . loco 'irrogetur' perfecte explicatur."—*Apollinaris*, VI (1933), 343.

[75] Canon 2244, § 3. Censura *ab homine* multiplicatur, si *plura praecepta* plures sententiae vel *plures distinctae partes eiusdem praecepti* aut sententiae suam quaeque censuram *infligant*. (Italics not in original text.)

[76] Canon 2244, § 2. Censura *latae sententiae* multiplicatur:

1°: Si diversa delicta, quorum singula censuram secumferunt, eadem vel distincta actione committantur;

2°. Si idem delictum, censura punitum, pluries repetatur ita ut *plura sint delicta distincta;*

3°. Si delictum, diversis censuris a distinctis Superioribus punitum, semel aut pluries committatur. (Italics not in original text.)

The reason why the term *"latae sententiae"* is used, and not the term *"a iure,"* is this: all *ferendae sententiae* determined censures which are also determined by the common law are *a iure* before their infliction and become *ab homine* only after the infliction; moreover, the term *"latae sententiae"* connotes penalties attached either by law or by precept, while the term *a iure* precludes penalties attached by precept. Cf. *infra*, p. 103.

ticularis, asserts that from the order of the division of censures given in canon 2245, it is obvious that in the fourth paragraph of the canon in question the term *a iure* is logically to be supplied.[77] Kinane's argument is: the first paragraph simply states that censures are either reserved or not reserved; the second paragraph treats of censures inflicted *ab homine* and begins to treat of censures determined *a iure;* the third paragraph deals with censures derived *a iure* without mentioning that they are derived *a iure* and without mentioning how they are brought about; therefore he concludes that in paragraph four censures derived *a iure* logically constitute the subject-matter; otherwise the whole canon is haphazard, incomplete, and illogical. Since in the third paragraph the term *a iure* is omitted, its similar omission in paragraph four is not unusual or unexpected.

The following remarks may be made in reference to Kinane's argument: If the structure of canon 2245 is carefully studied, the omission of the term *a iure* in the third paragraph is not unusual or unexpected, but rather self-explanatory, for after the end of the preceding paragraph, wherein censures reserved *a iure* were precisely divided into censures reserved to the ordinary and censures reserved to the Holy See, paragraph three explicitly refers to the preceding paragraph when it begins with the phrase *"E reservatis Apostolicae Sedi."* Paragraph four begins without any reference to the preceding paragraph. Apart from this implication, it is to be remembered that Michiels does consider paragraph four to refer to censures derived *tamquam a iure* (excluding *ferendae sententiae* censures determined by the law after the sentence is inflicted).

According to Michiels and Roberti *latae sententiae* contracted censures which are attached to particular precepts are derived *tamquam a iure.* The fact that *ferendae sententiae* censures when they are not imposed by precept, also derive *a iure* before their infliction is not the only reason for the use in canon 2245, § 4 of the term *"latae sententiae"* instead of the term *"a iure"* for

[77] "The Reservation of Censures 'Latae Sententiae' Imposed by a Particular Precept"—*IER,* XL (1932), 534; Beste (*Introductio in Codicem,* pp. 903, 904), proposes the same argument. Cf. also Ayrinhac, *Penal Legislation,* p. 64.

canon 2245, § 4, uses the phrase "*nisi in lege vel praecepto*," and the use of the word "precept" precludes *a iure* derived censures, as is clear from the definition of *a iure* derived censures as furnished in canon 2217, § 1, 3°.[78] Therefore, there remains no doubt that paragraph four of canon 2245 refers to all *latae sententiae* determined censures.

Vermeersch-Creusen offer against Michiels' views another objection which has not been discussed thus far. Vermeersch-Creusen state that in the decree of the Sacred Congregation of the Council of October 24, 1922, the *latae sententiae* determined censure which was attached to a particular and general precept by the decree is considered as *ab homine*.[79] The response, however, does not prove the existence of an *ab homine* inflicted censure which is at the same time *latae sententiae*. It will suffice to cite the text in question. The text reads:

> Nonostante che il sac. Gaetano Gliozzo sia stato da questa S. Congregazione del Concilio prima sospesso e poi dichiarato irregolare per violata censura, e finalmente anche rimosso dalla parrocchia di Ficarra, in diocesi di Patti, con rispettivi decreti 8 febbraio, 6 marzo e 5 aprile 1922, tuttavia egli ha osato continuare nell'esercizio del sacro ministero e dell'ufficio parrocchiale, mettendosi così in aperta ribellione con l'autorità ecclesiastica ed impendendone inoltre l'escercizio della relativa guirisdizione.
>
> Allo scopo pertanto di riparare al pubblico scandalo e di richiamare l'infelice sacerdote e sensi di resipiscenza, questa S. Congregazione del Concilio *con il presente decreto infligge al predetto Sac. Gaetano Gliozzo la scommunica* speciali modo riservata alla Santa Sede, da contrarsi anche da coloro che comunicassero in divinis con il medesimo sacerdote. (Italics not in the original text.)[80]

The excommunication inflicted by the particular precept is of a *ferendae sententiae* character for continued contumacy; the ex-

---

[78] (Poena dicitur): *A iure,* si poena determinata *in ipsa lege* statuatur, sive latae sententiae sit sive ferendae. (Latter Italics not in original text.)

[79] Cf. Vermeersch-Creusen, *Epitome,* III, n. 406.

[80] AAS, XIV (1922), 594-595.

communication threatened by the general precept is of a *latae sententiae* character only.

Roberti[81] affirms the opinion of Michiels. Since Roberti's arguments are essentially the same as those of Michiels, it will be sufficient to treat only those points which add to the ones already proposed and discussed by Michiels. Roberti calls the reader's attention to the Constitution *"Si unquam,"*[82] which, in granting faculties to confessors to absolve from censures, implies that an *ab homine* censure requires the intervention of a judge. He also answers a possible objection which could arise in one's consideration of the division of penalties as given by the Code. The Code does not mention precepts *ad instar legis* in canon 2217, § 1, 3°, although it does speak of them in § 1, 1°, 2° of the same canon. According to Roberti the lacuna is easily supplied from the general principle that precepts imposed *ad instar legis* are to be likened to laws themselves.[83] The silence of the Code is explained as traceable to the old law in which the precept imposed *ad instar legis* was scarcely considered, since the juridical concept of delicts was not precisely determined before the Code.[84]

After the consideration of these various opinions it is apparent that authors are divided into four groups.

1. Michiels and Roberti assert that a *latae sententiae* censure attached to any precept is not reserved either before or after a declaratory sentence unless the reservation be expressly stated, since it is derived not *ab homine* but *tamquam a iure.*

2. Creusen maintains that a *latae sententiae* censure, but only when it is attached to a particular precept, is always reserved

---

[81] "An censura latae sententiae per praeceptum constituta sit reservata?" *Apollinaris,* VI (1933), 341-348.

[82] Pius XI, const. *"Si unquam,"* 15 iul. 1924: ". . . concedimus, ut per Annum Sanctum possint . . . absolvere quoslibet poenitentes non solum a quibusvis censuris et peccatis Romano Pontifici aut Ordinario a iure reservatis, sed etiam a censura *ab homine* seu *a quovis iudice lata,* cuius tamen absolutio in foro externo non suffragabitur"—*AAS,* XVI (1924), 310. (Italics not in the original text.)

[83] Canon 2195, § 2. Nisi ex adiunctis aliud appareat, quae dicuntur de delictis, applicantur etiam violationibus praecepti cui poenalis sanctio adnexa sit.

[84] *Art. cit.—Apollinaris,* VI (1933), 343.

even before a declaratory sentence, since it is to be considered as deriving *ab homine.* Ayrinhac, Beste, Blat, Cerato, Chelodi, Cipollini, Cocchi, Coronata, Crnica, Ferreres, Kinane, Moriarty, Noldin and Prümmer likewise consider such a censure as deriving *ab homine,* but Ayrinhac, Cocchi, Coronata and Moriarty admit the existence of a *dubium iuris.* Beste states that superiors should be clear when they impose a precept in order that every issue of doubt may be precluded.

3. Sole and Salucci hold that a *latae sententiae* censure attached to any precept is not reserved unless it is expressly so stated in the precept, but that it is reserved even before any declaratory sentence has been pronounced, if express mention of the reservation has accompanied the giving of the precept.

4. Cappello and De Meester state that a *latae sententiae* censure attached to a particular precept is not reserved before a declaratory sentence has been pronounced unless that be so stated in the precept, but that it is reserved, upon a declaratory sentence, to the one who declared the sentence.

The final conclusion relative to the discussion of this entire chapter can be stated as follows: A *latae sententiae* incurred censure which is attached to a particular precept is to be considered *tamquam a iure* and as a consequence is not reserved unless the reservation is explicitly stated by the author of the censure. The reasons which militate for the adherence to this conclusion are: First, this conclusion satisfactorily establishes harmony between the texts of canons 2217, § 1, 2°; 2245, § 4, and 2244, §2, 2°, and between the texts of canons 2217, § 1, 3°; 2245, §2, and 2244, § 3. Second, this conclusion interprets the texts of the just mentioned canons according to the strict interpretation of the fourth paragraph of canon 2245.

CHAPTER VI

Ignorance in Regard to the Reservation of Censures

A. ignorance in general

Ignorance in general is the lack of knowledge concerning a certain thing. It denotes therefore an habitual state of mind. Ignorance differs from error, which, as the assent of the mind to something not in conformity with the truth, besides the lack of knowledge involves a judgment to the contrary. Ignorance differs from inadvertence inasmuch as in the latter the mind, although habitually it has a knowledge of the thing, does not actually attend to the thing. Ignorance, which denotes an habitual state of the mind, is here understood as actual ignorance.[1] Ignorance in the canonical sense includes inadvertence, forgetfulness, distraction and error, since the Code considers them equal and does not go into any distinctions.[2]

B. ignorance on the part of the confessor

If the confessor who does not possess faculties to absolve from reserved censures and who is ignorant of the law which establishes the reservation of the censure, absolves from the censure and the sin, the absolution of the censure is valid; but an exception is made by the Code which rules out the validity of the absolution for censures inflicted *ab homine* and censures reserved *specialissimo modo* to the Holy See.[3] On the part of the con-

[1] Cappello, *De Censuris*, n. 48.

[2] Canon 2202, § 3. Cf. also Cappello, *loc. cit.* and *ibid.*, n. 73; Cerato, *Censurae Vigentes*, n. 31, 2°; Beste, *Introductio in Codicem*, p. 905; Coronata, *Institutiones Iuris Canonici*, IV, 167.

[3] Canon 2247, § 3. Si confessarius, ignorans reservationem, poenitentem a censura ac peccato absolvat, absolutio censurae valet, dummodo ne sit censura ab homine aut censura specialissimo modo Sedi Apostolicae reservata.

fessor no ignorance of the reservation of *ab homine* or *specialissimo modo* reserved censures can render the absolution valid. The canon dealing with ignorance of the reservation of censures specifies the *confessarius* as the passive subject of the ignorance and refers to the internal sacramental forum only, since this is implied in the preceding words "*confessarius*" and "*a censura ac peccato absolvat,*" even though by way of general rule any jurisdiction granted for the internal forum can be used also in the internal *extrasacramental* forum, unless the sacramental forum is expressly determined as a condition for the use of such jurisdiction.[4] Further, the canon speaks of ignorance in general on the part of the confessor and thereby includes culpable ignorance, even crass or supine.[5] If absolution is granted according to the norm of this canon, and later either the confessor, or the penitent, or both, learn that a reserved censure had been incurred, neither is obliged to do anything, since the absolution was direct.[6]

The prescriptions of canon 2247, § 3, apply, even when there exists ignorance, inadvertence, forgetfulness, distraction or error in reference to the reservation alone. The confessor may be fully aware of the existence of the censure, e.g., he may well know that an excommunication is attached to the sin of apostasy, but he may through ignorance, inadvertence, etc., think that this excommunication is not reserved and hence grant absolution, while in reality the excommunication is reserved *speciali modo* to the Pope. That the ignorance of the confessor does not invalidate the absolution from certain definite classes of reserved censures is entirely new legislation in the Code.[7]

---

[4] Canon 202, § 2. Potestas collata pro foro interno exerceri potest etiam in foro interno extra-sacramentali, *nisi sacramentale exigatur.*

Cf. Blat, *De Delictis et Poenis,* p. 104.

[5] Cf. Ayrinhac, *Penal Legislation,* p. 67; Blat, *loc. cit.;* Cappello, *loc. cit.;* Coronata, *loc. cit.;* De Meester, *Juris Canonici et Juris Canonico-Civilis Compendium,* III, n. 1740.

[6] Cf. Cappello, *loc. cit.;* Coronata, *loc. cit.;* Beste, *loc. cit.;* Cerato, *Censurae Vigentes,* n. 16, 7ª; De Meester, *loc. cit.*

[7] Cf. Ayrinhac, *loc. cit.;* Cappello, *ibid.,* n. 73, note 22; Coronata, *loc. cit.;* De Meester, *loc. cit.;* Vermeersch-Creusen, *Epitome,* III, 446. Cf. also the pre-Code author D'Annibale (1815-1892) (*Summula Theologiae Moralis,* I, n. 343), who stated absolutely: "Nam, si inferior absolvit ignarus reserva-

The words *"poenitentem a censura ac peccato absolvat"* seem to refer to the general formula of the absolution, and not to the validity of the absolution from sins.[8] This will be more clearly understood when the effects of the disposition of the penitent upon the absolution from censures are considered. The question is: If the penitent knows that the confessor lacks the necessary faculties to absolve from a reserved censure, and that the confessor is ignorant of the reservation, but nevertheless obtains absolution, is that absolution valid?

Coronata asserts briefly that the absolution is in and of itself valid.[9] Other authors say that the absolution is valid, provided that the penitent has the proper dispositions.[10] Cappello distinguishes; the absolution of the censure is always valid; the absolution from the sins is valid if, notwithstanding his knowledge of the confessor's ignorance, the penitent has the proper dispositions, e.g., if the penitent thinks that he is not sinning, or at least not gravely. Otherwise the absolution from the sins would be invalid.[11]

Blat, in contradiction to the above-mentioned authors, maintains that the very knowledge of the reservation on the part of the penitent invalidates the absolution from the censure.[12] The

---

tionis *procul dubio* nihil agit." Other pre-Code authors such as Reiffenstuel, Schmalzgrueber, Devoti, Craisson, Wernz and Lega do not deal with the ignorance of the reservation on the part of the confessor.

[8] Cerato, however (*loc. cit.*) simply states that the words, "D. N. I. Ch. te absolvat et ego auctoritate Ipsius te absolvo *ab omni vinculo excommunicationis* (*suspensionis*) *et interdicti*, in quantum possum et tu indiges," which are to be used by every confessor in absolving any penitent even from sins only, then take on a fuller reason and deeper sense, when the penitent, possessing the proper dispositions, is absolved by the general form of the absolution from the sins he confessed and from possible censures of which he is unaware.

[9] *Institutiones Iuris Canonici, loc. cit.*

[10] Cf. Vermeersch-Creusen, *loc. cit.;* Cocchi, *Commentarium in Codicem Iuris Canonici*, VIII, 113; Salucci, *Diritto Penale*, p. 207; Cerato, *loc. cit.*

[11] *De Censuris, loc. cit.* Cf. also Ayrinhac, *loc. cit.;* De Meester, *loc. cit.*

[12] *Ibid.*, p. 105. Vermeersch-Creusen, Cocchi, Salucci and Cerato do not explicitly state that the very knowledge of the reservation on the part of the penitent would affect his proper disposition for a valid absolution, for the penitent could think that he is not sinning, or at least not sinning gravely, when under these circumstances he is asking for absolution from a sin to which a reserved censure is attached.

reason which he alleges does not seem to have any foundation in the law.[13] The fact that the disposition of the penitent in a given case would not affect the validity of the absolution from the censure could be provided for by positive legislation, which would not thereby encourage malicious deceit. Such positive legislation would in such a case consider the legal or juridical effect, and simply abstract from the moral issue involved, as it clearly does, for instance, in canon 1054.[14]

In answering Blat's view, one notes first that canon 2247, § 3, mentions only the ignorance of the confessor, and says nothing about the ignorance or knowledge of the penitent. The knowledge of the penitent would seem, therefore, not to interfere with the fulfilling of the conditions set by the law in canon 2247, § 3.[15] It seems that the absolution from the censure (excluding *ab homine* and *specialissimo modo* reserved censures) will always be valid. The canon reads: if the confessor who is ignorant of the censure's reservation by the law absolves the penitent *"a censura ac peccato,"* the *"absolutio censurae"* is valid. The canon makes no mention of the absolution of the sin. Thus it may be inferred that the validity of the absolution from sins does not enter into the question with which this canon is concerned.

But the confessor who, while fully knowing that he lacks the necessary jurisdiction, would dare to absolve from reserved sins (not censures) would incur *ipso facto* a suspension from hearing confessions;[16] and if he would knowingly absolve without faculties from a *latae sententiae* incurred excommunication which is reserved *speciali* or *specialissimo modo* to the Holy See, he would incur an excommunication reserved *simpliciter* to the Holy See.[17]

---

[13] *Loc. cit.*: "Tunc enim deest poenitenti debita dispositio, cum in factor recipiendae absolutionis peccet contra legislatoris reservantis voluntatem. Et quia praescriptum canonis prospicit validitati absolutionis a peccato, deest mens extendendi illud ad casum propositum. Insuper fraus et dolus, sicut in casu, nemini patrocinari debet."

[14] Dispensatio a minore impedimento concessa, nullo sive obreptionis sive subreptionis vitio irritatur, etsi unica causa finalis in precibus exposita falsa fuerit.

[15] Cf. Cappello, *loc. cit.*

[16] Canon 2366.

[17] Canon 2338.

It is clear that in either case the absolution from the censure would be invalid, since the confessor then would be acting against the will of the legislator who determined through canon 2247, § 3, to grant jurisdiction only in case of ignorance on the part of the confessor.

C. IGNORANCE ON THE PART OF THE PENITENT

If the penitent does not incur a censure because of ignorance,[18] it is clear that the reservation of the sin also does not exist.[19] The ignorance, however, which is here under discussion is ignorance not of the censure but of the reservation itself. It is presupposed, therefore, that the penitent knows well that he has incurred a censure, but does not know that the censure is reserved. Two questions have to be solved in reference to this kind of ignorance, namely, 1) does the mere ignorance of the reservation excuse one from incurring the censure? 2) does the ignorance of the reservation excuse one from the reservation itself, so that any confessor may absolve from the incurred censure?

To the first question the following answer must be made: it is clear that mere ignorance of the reservation itself does not excuse one from incurring the censure.[20] Swoboda asserts that error or ignorance about the reservation which is attached to a penalty cannot be considered a substantial mistake in regard to the penalty and, therefore, does not fall under the provisions of canon 2229.[21] If one is aware of the fact that a certain crime is punished with a censure, but is ignorant merely of the fact that there is a reservation attached to the censure, he is not excused from incurring that censure, for he who consents to the punishment of the censure implicitly consents to the reservation

---

[18] Canon 2229.

[19] Canon 2246, § 3 . . . verum si quis a censura *excusatur* vel ab eadem fuit absolutus, reservatio peccati penitus cessat. (Italics not in the original text.)

[20] Cf. Coronata, *Institutiones Iuris Canonici,* IV, 160, 161.

[21] *Ignorance in Relation to the Imputability of Delicts*, p. 226. Cf. also Marc-Gestermann-Raus, *Institutiones,* II, n. 1770.

and all the other effects, even though he is ignorant of these effects.[22] Evidently a penitent who knows he has incurred a reserved censure but is ignorant only of the precise manner of its reservation can not be excused either from the censure or from the reservation, for then the knowledge of the censure and its reservation is even clearer and more comprehensive than in the immediately preceding case.[23] An example of this kind of ignorance is the ignorance of one who knows that he has incurred a censure reserved to the Holy See, but is ignorant whether the censure is reserved *simpliciter* or *speciali modo* to the Holy See.

In answer to the second proposed question the following may be said: Ignorance of the reservation itself does not excuse from the reservation, since reservation can not be considered penal in nature.[24] Cappello declines to solve this question in practice, although he leaves little probability for the opposite opinion of those authors who consider reservation penal in nature and therefore regard ignorance of the reservation as a cause excusing from the reservation.[25]

Thus far canon 2247, § 3 was considered without any relation to canon 2249, § 2 in which the confessor is ignorant of a reserved censure, since the penitent has concealed the case. The penitent may conceal the reserved censure in good or bad faith; good and bad faith on the part of the penitent produce different effects on the operation of canon 2249, § 2. If the penitent is inculpably ignorant of the necessity of confessing a certain reserved censure, he is said to be in good faith. Culpable ignorance would exclude good faith, which requires that the penitent be properly disposed according to the principles of Moral Theology. The question of the relation of canon 2247, § 3 to canon 2249, § 2 will receive added treatment in the following section.

---

[22] Marc-Gestermann-Raus, *loc. cit.;* cf. also Lehmkuhl, *Theologia Moralis,* III, 295, 7.

[23] Cf. Cappello, *De Censuris,* n. 72.

[24] Cf. *supra,* pp. 24-25. There it is concluded that the opinion which adheres to the penal nature of reservation can not be considered probable.

[25] Cappello (*loc. cit.*) says: "Speculative loquendo, nobis *vera* sententia est, quae affirmat poenitentem teneri reservatione, etsi illam ignoraverit. Ratio est, quia fundamentum contrariae opinionis, nimirum quod reservatio sit *poena,* verius iure antiquo et certe iure Codicis . . . . non exsistit."

D. GOOD FAITH AND BAD FAITH ON THE PART OF THE CONFESSOR AND THE PENITENT

If the penitent in good faith should confess his sins to a confessor who has faculties to absolve from reserved censures, but should forget to confess the sin to which a censure is attached, he could thereafter confess that sin to any confessor, because the censure which was connected with the sin is considered to have been removed by the confessor who had the necessary faculties, though the sin itself was absolved only indirectly.[26] This extends not only to the confessor who has a special mandate or particular faculties, but also includes the confessor who acquires faculties in virtue of canon 2247, § 3;[27] this rule applies to all censures with the exception of censures reserved *specialissimo modo* to the Holy See and censures inflicted *ab homine*. However, censures inflicted *ab homine* are governed by canon 2249, § 2, since canon 2249, §§ 1, 2 treats of censures in general and does not limit itself to censures determined *a iure*.[28] Woywod, on the contrary, asserts that the rule of canon 2249 has reference only to censures which are *a iure*, for, he argues, censures inflicted *ab homine* are always reserved to the superior who inflicted the same.[29] The fact, namely, that censures inflicted *ab homine* are reserved to the superior who inflicted the same, can not be denied, but does not prove his assertion.

All censures reserved *a iure* are reserved to the one who enacted the reservation or to the one to whom the superior reserves the

---

[26] Canon 2249, § 2. Cf. also Coronata, *Institutiones Iuris Canonici*, IV, 167; Salucci, *Diritto Penale*, p. 204.

[27] Coronata, *loc. cit.*; Cappello, *De Censuris*, n. 73, 5°. Cappello (*loc. cit.*) clearly distinguishes between the validity of the absolution from censures and the validity of the absolutions from sins. Cf. also *supra*, pp. ? ?.

[28] Canon 2249, § 1. Si quis pluribus censuris detineatur, potest ab una absolvi, ceteris minime absolutis.

§ 2. Petens absolutionem, debet casus omnes indicare, secus absolutio valet tantum pro casu expresso; quod si absolutio, quamvis particularis petitio facta sit, fuerit generalis, valet quoque pro reticitis bona fide, excepta censura specialissimo modo Sedi Apostolicae reservata, non autem pro reticitis mala fide.

[29] *A Practical Commentary*, II, n. 2090.

censure;[80] all *ab homine* inflicted censures are reserved to him who inflicted the censure or passed the judicial sentence, or to his competent superior, or his successor, or his delegate.[81] By a liberal concession of canon 2249 the absolution which is granted in the general form by one having faculties in relation to the reserved censures and which at the same time is received by one who has forgotten by mistake one or other of the censures is valid. Censures reserved *specialissimo modo* to the Holy See and those concealed in bad faith are not included in this concession. The logical conclusion, therefore, is *ab homine* inflicted censures are not excluded from this concession. It is necessary, however, that the person petition one who has the proper faculties to absolve from the incurred censures, and according to canons 2245, § 2 and 2253, 2° the one competent to absolve from *ab homine* inflicted censures is he who inflicted the censure, or his superior, or his successor, or his delegate.

A precise distinction, therefore, must be made between the operation of canon 2247, § 3 and that of canon 2249, § 2. The former presupposes the initial absence of jurisdiction in reference to the reserved censures, while the latter presupposes the possession of proper faculties. Further, canon 2247, § 3 formally treats of the ignorance on the part of the confessor and operates regardless of the bad faith on the part of the penitent, while canon 2249, § 2, formally treats of the concealment of censures in good faith on the part of the penitent or petitioner. Canon 2247, § 3, then, can be employed in the internal sacramental forum, while canon 2249, § 2, is not limited to the internal forum, but may be used in the external forum also.

Despite the fact that the absolution granted according to the legislation of canon 2247, § 3, is valid also for those cases which were concealed in good faith, nevertheless there exist two exceptions, namely, censures inflicted *ab homine* and censures reserved *specialissimo modo* to the Holy See, and not only the one exception, namely, censures reserved *specialissimo modo* to the *Holy See*, which exception is made in canon 2249, § 2. Canon 2249, § 2, applies in canon 2247, § 3, only in as much as canon 2247, § 3,

---

[80] Canon 2253, 3°.

[81] Canons 2245, § 2; 2253, 2°.

extends faculties to the confessor who is ignorant of the reservation. Canon 2247, § 3 does not extend faculties to absolve from *ab homine* reserved censures. Therefore, the rule of canon 2249, § 2, which presupposes the possession of the proper faculties to absolve from reserved censures, and in no way intends to grant faculties to those who are lacking them does not annul the exception which is explicitly mentioned in canon 2247, § 3, in regard to *ab homine* inflicted censures.

Absolution from *ab homine* reserved censures granted according to canon 2249, § 2, is valid only when the one who absolves has the jurisdiction to do so in accord with the rule of canon 2253, 2°. Absolution from *ab homine* inflicted censures granted according to canon 2247, § 3, is not valid, regardless of whether the penitent is in good faith.

It is disputed among the authors whether the penitent, if he possesses the proper dispositions, is absolved validly and directly from the sin reserved by reason of a censure which is either *ab homine* or *specialissimo modo* when the absolution is granted by a confessor who is ignorant of the reservation and who does not possess special faculties in relation to the mentioned reserved censures. Coronata[32] in opposition to other authors,[33] maintains that the absolution from the sin is valid regardless of whether or not the reserved sin is the only sin confessed. De Meester, Cappello, Vermeersch-Creusen and Beste assert that, if the penitent confesses only the sin reserved by reason of a censure incurred *ab homine* or *specialissimo modo,* then the absolution from the sin is invalid, as is the absolution from the censure. In their view there is no doubt that the absolution from the censure is invalid because of the lack of jurisdiction,[34] and that the censure binds until absolution from it is received.[35]

All authors also agree that if bad faith intervenes either on the part of the confessor or on the part of the penitent, then the

[32] *Op. cit.,* IV, pp. 170, 172, notes 2, 5.

[33] De Meester, *Juris Canonici et Juris Canonico-Civilis Compendium,* III, 178; note 3; Cappello, *De Censuris,* n. 107; Vermeersch-Creusen, *Epitome,* III, n. 449; Beste, *Introductio in Codicem,* p. 905.

[34] Canon 872.

[35] Canon 2248, § 1. Quaelibet censura, semel contracta, tollitur tantum legitima absolutione.

absolution from the censure is invalid in those cases in which only the *ab homine* or *specialissimo modo* reserved censure is confessed. Finally, all authors agree that, if a sin to which is attached a censure reserved *specialissimo modo* or *ab homine* is confessed together with other non-reserved sins, then the absolution granted in bad faith but received by a penitent possessing good faith is direct in reference to the non-reserved sins, and indirect in reference to the reserved sin.[36]

Thus there remains a difference of opinion only in reference to the validity of the absolution from the sin in those cases in which good faith is present on the part of both the penitent and the confessor, who lacks jurisdiction in regard to reserved censures and the sin which is reserved *ab homine* or *specialissimo modo* is the only sin confessed. The opinion of Coronata does not lack probability, if the text of canon 2247, § 3, is considered in connection with the declaration of Pope Paul IV.[37] Jurisdiction is granted by Pope Paul IV to absolve directly from any sin reserved *ratione censurae* in cases of ignorance; the Code does not contradict this concession, for the Code speaks only of the validity or invalidity of the absolution from the censure, and invalidates only the absolution from *ab homine* or *specialissimo modo* reserved censures which is granted in good faith or in ignorance, but not necessarily the absolution from the sin.[38]

[36] Coronata, *op. cit.,* IV, pp. 167, 173; De Meester, *loc. cit.;* Cappello, *ibid.,* n. 107, 4°, 5°.

[37] "Notanda declaratio quae sequitur. In Congreg. S. Officii die 10 Sept. 1556.—SS. mus D.N. (Paulus PP. IV). . . , ad consulendum quieti conscientiarum christifidelium, declaravit et concessit, quod si de cetero contingat aliquem ad sacramentum Confessionis accedere quacumque ecclesiastica censura innodatum, quam et ipse et confessarius penitus ignorent, beneficium absolutionis ab eodem confessario consequi possit et consequatur, perinde ac si nullo Ecclesiae vinculo esset innodatus; et casu quo postea de huiusmodi censura ipsum sic absolutum notitiam habere contingat, non teneatur peccata tempore ignorantiae huiusmodi iam confessa de novo confiteri, neque novam absolutionem de eisdem peccatis quaerere et consequi, sed, absolutione peccatorum iam obtenta, quietus absolutionem ab excommunicatione, cuius notitia sibi supervenit, quaerere teneatur."—*Collectanea Sacrae Congregationis de Propaganda Fide,* II, 216 in nota (n. 1658).

[38] Canon 2247, § 3. Si confessarius, ignorans reservationem, poenittentem a censura ac peccato absolvat, *absolutio censurae valet, dummodo ne sit censura* ab homine aut censura specialissimo modo Sedi Apostolicae reservata. (Italics not in the original text.)

Therefore it seems possible to have a direct absolution of sin even apart from the valid absolution of the reserved censure attached to that sin in the case of *ab homine* or of *specialissimo modo* reserved censures, provided only that the confessor and the penitent are both in good faith.

E. SUMMARY OF THE EFFECTS OF GOOD AND BAD FAITH ON THE PART OF THE PENITENT UPON THE ABSOLUTION GRANTED ACCORDING TO CANON 2247, § 3

To understand the present summary it is necessary to keep in mind the principles which are used in the solution of the various possible combinations of good and bad faith on the part of the penitent. By force of canon 2247, § 3, a confessor who is ignorant of a reservation obtains jurisdiction to absolve validly from all reserved censures with the exception of *ab homine* and *specialissimo modo* reserved censures. Now, if the penitent confesses to such a confessor and conceals in good faith one or the other reserved censure, the absolution is valid in reference to all except *ab homine* and *specialissimo modo* reserved censures.

The cases which may occur in the operation of canon 2249, § 2, are not considered, for this canon makes a single exception for *specialissimo modo* reserved censures, while the absolution from *ab homine* reserved censures the mention of which a penitent or a petitioner has concealed in good faith is valid, provided that the confessor or the one who is petitioned has jurisdiction to absolve from these *ab homine* reserved censures according to canon 2253, 2°. This rule would not apply to the confessor who by virtue of canon 2247, § 3, obtains jurisdiction to absolve from certain reserved censures in the internal sacramental forum.

In the following six instances consideration is given only to the absolution from *ab homine* and *specialissimo modo* reserved censures.

1. If the absolution is granted in good faith on the part of the confessor and is simultaneously received in good faith on the part of the penitent, then the absolution is valid and direct in regard to the sins confessed, regardless of whether the sins which are reserved by reason of these censures (i.e., reserved *ab*

homine and *specialissimo modo*) are the only sins confessed; indirect in regard to sins forgotten in good faith; invalid in regard to all these censures (i.e., reserved *ab homine* and *specialissimo modo*).

2. If the absolution is granted in good faith on the part of the confessor but is received in bad faith on the part of the penitent, then the absolution is invalid both in regard to the sins and in regard to the censures (i.e., reserved *ab homine* and *specialissimo modo*), when only these censures (i.e., reserved *ab homine* and *specialissimo modo*) or sins reserved because of these same censures were confessed.

3. If the absolution is granted in bad faith on the part of the confessor, but is received in good faith on the part of the penitent, then the absolution is invalid both in regard to the sins and in regard to the censures (i.e., reserved *ab homine* and *specialissimo modo*), when only these censures (i.e., reserved *ab homine* and *specialissimo modo*) or sins reserved because of these same censures were confessed.

4. If the absolution is granted in good faith on the part of the confessor but is received in bad faith on the part of the penitent, then the absolution is invalid in regard to both these censures (i.e., reserved *ab homine* and *specialissimo modo*) and all sins, even though sins other than such as are reserved because of these censures (i.e., reserved *ab homine* and *specialissimo modo*) were confessed. The validity of the absolution from other kinds of reserved censures would not be called into question by this rule (refer below for rules which govern censures not reserved *ab homine* or *specialissimo modo*).

5. If the absolution is granted in bad faith on the part of the confessor but is received in good faith on the part of the penitent who confesses together with these reserved sins other non-reserved sins, the absolution is invalid in regard to the censures; valid and direct in regard to the non-reserved sins; valid and indirect in regard to the sins reserved because of the censures.

6. If the absolution is granted in bad faith on the part of the confessor and is simultaneously received in bad faith on the part of the penitent, the absolution is invalid in regard to both all censures and all sins.

In the following instances consideration is given to the absolution from all other reserved censures which are reserved neither *ab homine* nor *specialissimo modo*.

1. If the absolution is granted in good faith on the part of the confessor and is simultaneously received in good faith on the part of the penitent, the absolution is valid and direct in regard to the sins confessed; is indirect in regard to sins concealed in good faith; is valid in regard to censures (except *ab homine* and *specialissimo modo* reserved censures), even though the sin reserved because of the censure is the only sin confessed. The absolution is also valid in regard to censures (except, of course, *ab homine* and *specialissimo modo* reserved censures) which the penitent has concealed in good faith.

2. If the absolution is granted in good faith on the part of the confessor but is received in bad faith on the part of the penitent, the absolution is valid in regard to the censures (except *ab homine* and *specialissimo modo* reserved censures) but is invalid in regard to the sins, even though sins other than the ones reserved because of the censures are confessed.

3. If the absolution is granted in bad faith on the part of the confessor but is received in good faith on the part of the penitent, then the absolution is invalid in regard to the censures, but valid in regard to the sins, when a sin other than the sins reserved because of the censures is confessed. The absolution in the case would be direct in regard to the non-reserved sin and indirect in regard to the reserved sins.

4. If the absolution is granted in bad faith on the part of the confessor and is simultaneously received in bad faith on the part of the penitent, the absolution is invalid in regard to both censures and sins.

It must be remembered that, if the confessor should have jurisdiction in relation to *ab homine* reserved censures by reason of canon 2253, 2°, the absolution granted to a penitent who happens to conceal one or other of these censures in good faith is to be considered valid according to canon 2249, § 2. This applies to the external forum also. Such could not be the case in the instances considered above, for in all those instances the rule of canon 2247, § 3 alone would be operative, inasmuch as the non-possession of jurisdiction in relation to the reserved censures on the part of the confessor is inherently postulated in such cases.

CONCLUSIONS

1. Reservation of its essence is neither penal nor medicinal; the purpose intended by the superior for enacting a reservation may be either penal or medicinal, as the nature of the case leaves it possible, but the Code itself does not actualize the possibility of a penal purpose.

2. The prohibition of canon 2247, § 1 by which an ordinary can not validly attach to a censure reserved to the Pope another censure reserved to himself extends to all three species of censures, namely, excommunications, suspensions and interdicts, although he may attach a censure which is not reserved.

3. The response of the Commission for the Interpretation of the Code which states that a *peregrinus* is bound by the reservations of the place in which he sojourns does not refer to the reservation of censures, and therefore, the *peregrinus* who has incurred an *a iure particulari* reserved censure in his own diocese can be absolved by any confessor while he sojourns in the extraneous diocese, even though a similar diocesan reserved censure exists in the extraneous diocese.

4. A *latae sententiae* determined censure which is attached to a particular precept is neither *a iure* nor *ab homine,* but is to be considered *tamquam a iure;* consequently, the incurred censure is not reserved, unless the one who imposes the precept expressly states that the censure is reserved.

5. Ignorance of the reservation, even crass or supine ignorance, on the part of the confessor does not stand in the way of the validity of the absolution granted for reserved censures as long as they are not *ab homine* inflicted or *specialissimo modo* reserved censures, regardless of whether the penitent knows that the confessor lacks proper jurisdiction in relation to the reserved censures.

6. The absolution granted by a confessor who has no jurisdiction to absolve from reserved censures is valid and direct in regard to the sins to which were added censures reserved *specialissimo modo* or inflicted *ab homine,* provided that the absolu-

tion was granted and received in good faith, even though the sins reserved in this manner are the only sins confessed.

7. The presence of bad faith on the part of the confessor who hasn't proper jurisdiction in reference to reserved censures stands in the way of the validity of the absolution granted for sins, if sins reserved because of either *ab homine* or *specialissimo modo* contracted censures are the only sins confessed.

8. The rule of canon 2249, § 2 does not annul the exception which is mentioned in canon 2247, § 3, in regard to *ab homine* inflicted censures, when the source of the confessor's jurisdiction is canon 2247, § 3; canon 2249, § 2, however, suffers only one exception, namely, *specialissimo modo* reserved censures, when the source of the confessor's jurisdiction is canon 2253, 2°.

BIBLIOGRAPHY

Sources

Acta Apostolicae Sedis, Commentarium Officiale, Romae, 1909-

Augustinus, Antonius, *Antiquae Decretalium Collectiones Commentariis et Emendationibus Illustratae,* Parisiis, 1621.

Bullarium Ssmi. Domini nostri Benedicti XIV, ed. nova, 13 vols., Mechliniae, 1826-1827.

Codex Iuris Canonici Pii X Pontificis Maximi iussu digestus Benedicti Papae XV auctoritate promulgatus, Romae: Typis Polyglottis Vaticanis, 1917.

Codicis Iuris Canonici Fontes cura Emi. Petri Card. Gasparri editi, 9 vols., Romae (postea Civitate Vaticana): Typis Polyglottis Vaticanis, 1923-1929. (Vols. VII, VIII, et IX ed. *cura et studio Emi. Iustiniani Card. Serédi.*)

Collectanea S. Congregationis de Propaganda Fide, 2 vols., Romae, 1907.

Corpus Iuris Canonici, ed. Lipsiensis 2. post Aemilii Ludovici Richter curas . . . instruxit Aemilius Friedberg, 2 vols., Lipsiae, 1879-1881.

Decretales D. Gregorii Papae IX, una cum Glossis Restitutae, Romae, 1582.

Decretum Gratiani Emendatum et Notationibus illustratum una cum Glossis, Romae, 1582.

Jaffé, Phillipus, *Regesta Pontificum Romanorum ab condita ecclesia ad annum post Christum natum 1198,* editionem 2. correctam et auctam auspiciis Gulielmi Wattenbach curaverunt S. Löwenfeld, F. Kaltenbrunner, P. Ewald, 2 vols. in 1, Lipsiae, 1885-1888.

Liber Sextus Decretalium, una cum Clementinis et Extravagantibus Earumque Glossis Restitutis, Romae, 1582.

Potthast, Augustus, *Regesta Pontificum Romanorum inde ab anno Post Christum Natum MCXCVIII ad annum MCCCIV,* 2 vols., Berolini, 1874-1875.

Schroeder, Henry J., *Canons and Decrees of the Council of Trent,* St. Louis, Herder, 1941.

Reference Works

Aertnys, Josephus, *Theologia Moralis juxta Doctrinam S. Alphonsi Mariae de Ligorio,* 5. ed., 2 vols., Tornaci: Casterman, 1898.

Alphonsus Ligouri, St., *Theologia Moralis,* ed. novissima, 10 vols. in 5, Mechliniae, 1852.

Arregui, Antonius, *Summarium Theologiae Moralis ad Recentem Codicem Iuris Canonici Accomodatum,* 10. ed., Bilbao: El Mensajero del Corazon de Jesus Apartado 73, 1927.

Ayrinhac, H. A., *Legislation on the Sacraments in the New Code of Canon Law,* New York: Longmans, Green and Co., 1928.

Ayrinhac, H. A., and Lydon, P. J., *Penal Legislation in the New Code of Canon Law,* revised edition, New York: Benziger, 1936.

Bachofen, Augustine Charles, *A Commentary on the New Code of Canon Law,* 8 vols., Vol. IV, 2. ed., 1921: *On the Sacraments (Except Matrimony) and Sacramentals;* Vol. VIII, 1922: *Penal Code,* St. Louis, Herder.

Ballerini, Antonius-Palmieri, Dominicus, *Opus Theologicum Morale,* 7 vols., Prati, 1889-1893.

Benedictus XIV, *De Synodo Dioecesana,* 2 vols., Venetiis, 1792.

Beste, Udalricus, *Introductio in Codicem,* Collegeville, Minn.: St. John's Abbey Press, 1938.

Blat, Albertus, *Commentarium Textus Codicis Iuris Canonici,* 6 vols., lib. II, *De Personis,* 2. ed., 1921; lib. III, *De Rebus,* Pars I, 1920; Partes II-VI, 1923; lib. V, *De Delictis et Poenis,* 1924, Romae.

Bonacina, Martinus, *Opera Omnia,* 3 vols., Venetiis, 1687.

Bucceroni, J., *Institutiones Theologiae Moralis secundum Doctrinam S. Thomae et S. Alphonsi,* 3. ed., 2 vols., Romae, 1898.

Cappello, Felix, *De Censuris iuxta Codicem Iuris Canonici,* 3. ed., Taurinorum Augustae: Marietti, 1933.

———, *Summa Iuris Publici Ecclesiastici ad Normam Codicis Iuris Canonici et Recentiorum S. Sedis Documentorum Concinnata,* 4. ed., Romae: Apud Aedes Universitatis Gregorianae, 1936.

Cerato, Prosdocimus, *Censurae Vigentes Ipso Facto a Codice Iuris Canonici Excerptae,* 2. ed., Patavii: Typis Seminarii, 1921.

Chelodi, Ioannes, *Ius Poenale et Ordo Procedendi in Iudiciis Criminalibus iuxta Codicem Iuris Canonici,* Tridenti: 1925 (1920?).

Cicognani, Hamletus J., *Ius Canonicum Primo Studii Anno in usum Auditorum Excerpta,* 2 vols. in 1, Romae, 1925.

———, *Canon Law,* 2. revised ed., authorized English version, translated by J. M. O'Hara and F. Brennan, Philadelphia: Dolphin Press, 1935.

Cipollini, Albertus D., *De Censuris Latae Sententiae iuxta Codicem Iuris Canonici,* Taurini: Marietti, 1925.

Clancy, Patrick M. J., *The Local Religious Superior,* The Catholic University of America Canon Law Studies, n. 175, Washington, D. C.: The Catholic University of America Press, 1943.

Cocchi, Guidus, *Commentarium in Codicem Iuris Canonici,* 2. ed., 8 vols., Taurinorum Augustae: Marietti, 1922-1930; Vol. VIII, *De Delictis et Poenis,* ed. 4., 1938.

Coronata, Mattheus Conte a, *Institutiones Iuris Canonici ad Usum Utriusque Cleri et Scholarum,* 5 vols., Taurini (Italia): Marietti, 1928-1936.

Craisson, D., *Manuale Totius Juris Canonici,* 5. ed., 4 vols., Pictavii, 1877.

Crnica, Antonius, *Modificationes in Tractatu de Censuris per Codicem Iuris Canonici Introductae,* S. Mauritii Agaunensis: Typis op. S. Augustini, 1919.

Croix, Claudius La, Theologia Moralis, 2 vols., Venetiis, 1722.

Dargin, Edward V., *Reserved Cases According to the Code of Canon Law,* The Catholic University of America Canon Law Studies, n. 20, Washington, D. C.: The Catholic University of America, 1924.

D'Annibale, Josephus, *Summula Theologiae Moralis,* 5. ed., 3 vols., Romae, 1908.

De Angelis, Philippus, *Praelectiones Juris Canonici ad Methodum Decretalium Gregorii IX Exactae,* 5. vols., Romae: Desclée, 1908; Vol. IV curavit Nazarenus Gentilini, 1891; Vols. I-V, 1880-1891.

De Meester, Alphonsus, *Juris Canonici et Juris Canonico-Civilis Compendium,* nova ed., 3 vols. in 4, Brugis: Desclée, 1921-1928.

Devoti, Joannis, *Institutionum Canonicarum Libri Quattuor,* 4 vols. in 2, Romae, 1829.

———, *Institutionum Canonicarum Libri Quattuor,* 4 vols. in 2, Leodii: H. Dessain, 1883.

Farrugia, Nicholaus, *De Casuum Conscientiae Reservatione iuxta Codicem Iuris Canonici,* 2. ed., Augustae Taurinorum-Romae, 1922.

Ferreres, Ioannes, *Institutiones Canonicae,* 2. ed., 2 vols., Barcinone: Subirana, 1920.

Genicot, Eduardus-Salsmans, I., *Institutiones Theologiae Moralis,* 10. ed., 2 vols., Bruxellis, 1922.

Gury, Joannes, et Ballerini, Antonius, *Compendium Theologiae Moralis,* 3. ed., 2 vols., Romae, 1874-1875.

Hammill, John L., *The Obligations of the Traveler According to Canon 14,* The Catholic University of America Canon Law Studies, n. 160, Washington, D. C.: The Catholic University of America Press, 1942.

Henricus Boich, *In Quinque Decretalium Libros Commentaria,* Venetiis, 1576.

Hollweck, Joseph, *Die kirchlichen Strafgesetze,* Mainz, 1899.

Hostiensis, Cardinalis (Henricus de Segusio), *Commentaria in Quinque Decretalium Libros,* 5 vols. in 3, Venetiis, 1581.

———, *Summa Aurea,* Venetiis, 1570.

Lega, Michael, *Praelectiones in Textum Iuris Canonici, De Delictis et Poenis,* 2. ed., Romae, 1910.

———, *Praelectiones in Textum Iuris Canonici, De Iudiciis Ecclesiasticis,* 4 vols., Romae, 1896-1901.

Lehmkuhl, Augustinus, *Theologia Moralis,* 6. ed., 2 vols., Friburgi Brisgoviae: Herder, 1890.

Lugo, Joannes de, *Disputationes Scholasticae et Morales,* ed. nova, 8 vols., Parisiis, 1868-1869.

Marc, Cl., Gestermann, Fr. X, et Raus, J. B., *Institutiones Morales Alphonsianae,* 18. ed., 2 vols., Lugduni: Vitte, 1927.

Maroto, Philippus, *Institutiones Iuris Canonici ad Normam Novi Codicis,* 2 vols., Tom. I, Matriti, 1919.

Maupied, Franciscus, L. M., *Juris Canonici Universi, per Faciliorem Methodum ad Veram Praxim Sincere Redacti Compendium,* 2 vols., Lutetiae: Parisiis, 1863.

Michiels, Gommarus, *Normae Generales Iuris Canonici, Commentarium Libri I Codicis Iuris Canonici,* 2 vols., Lublin: Universitas Catholica, 1929.

Moriarty, Francis E., *The Extraordinary Absolution from Censures,* The Catholic University of America Canon Law Studies, n. 113, Washington, D. C.: The Catholic University of America, 1938.

Mothon, Joseph, *Institutions Canoniques a l'usage des Curies Episcopales, du Clerge Paroissial, et des Familles Religieuses,* 2 vols., Societé Saint-Augustin: Desclée, 1924.

Noldin, H., *De Poenis Ecclesiasticis,* 3. and 4. ed., Oeniponte: Pustet, 1904.

Noldin, H., et Schmitt, A., *Summa Theologiae Moralis iuxta Codicem Iuris Canonici,* 23. ed., 3 vols., Oeniponte-Rauch: Pustet, 1935.

Noldin, H. — Schönegger, A., *De Censuris,* 29. ed., Oeniponte-Rauch: Pustet, 1935.

Ojetti, Benedictus, *Synopsis Rerum Moralium et Iuris Pontificii,* Romae, 1899.

Panormitanus, Abbas (Nicolaus de Tudeschis), *Commentaria in Quinque Libros Decretalium,* 5 vols. in 7, Venetiis, 1588.

Pennacchi, Josephus, *Commentaria in Constitutionem Apostolicae Sedis,* 2 vols., Romae, 1883.

Pignatelli, Giacomo, *Consultationes Canonicae,* 12 vols., Coloniae: Sumptibus Gabrielis et Samuelis De Tournes, 1700-1719.

Pirhing, Ernricus, *Jus Canonicum Nova Methodo Explicatum,* 5 vols. in 4, Dilingae, 1674—1678.

Prümmer, Dominicus, *Manuale Iuris Canonici in Usum Scholarum,* 3. ed., Friburgi Brisgoviae, 1922.

———, *Manulae Theologiae Moralis secundum Principia S. Thomae Aquinatis,* 4. and 5. ed., 3 vols., Friburgi Brisgoviae, 1928.

Rainer, Eligius G., *Suspension of Clerics,* The Catholic University of America Canon Law Studies, n. 111, Washington, D. C.: The Catholic University of America, 1937.

Raus, P. J. B., *Institutiones Canonicae Juxta Novum Codicem Juris pro Scholis vel ad Usum Privatum Synthetice Redactae,* ed. altera, Lugduni, Parisiis: Typis Emanuelis Vitte, 1931.

Raymond of Penyfort, St., *Summa,* ed. recognita et emendata, Veronae, 1744.

Reiffenstuel, Anacletus, *Jus Canonicum Universum,* 5 vols. in 7, Parisiis, 1864-1870.

Rufinus, *Summa Decretorum,* ed. Singer, Paderborn, 1902.

Salmanticenses, *Cursus Theologiae Moralis,* 6 vols. in 4, Venetiis, 1714-1728.

Salucci, Raffaele, *Il Diritto Penale secondo il Codice di Diritto Canonico,* 2 vols. in 1, Subiaco: Tipografia dei Monasteri, 1926-1930.

Sanchez, Thomas, *Opus Morale in Praecepta Decalogi,* 2 vols. in 1, Parmae, 1723.

———, *Disputationum de Sancto Matrimonio Tomi Tres,* 3 vols., Lugduni: Arisson, 1739.

Santi, Franciscus, *Praelectiones Juris Canonici juxta ordinem Decretalium Gregorii IX,* 2. ed., 5 vols. in 2, Ratisbonae: Pustet, 1886.

Schmalzgrueber, Franciscus, *Jus Ecclesiasticum Universum,* 5 vols. in 12, Romae, 1843-1845.

Shuhler, Ralph, *Privileges of Regulars to Absolve and Dispense,* The Catholic University of America Canon Law Studies, n. 186, Washington, D. C.: The Catholic University of America Press, 1943.

Sipos, Stephanus, *Enchiridion Iuris Canonici ad Usum Scholarum et Privatum,* Pécs ex Typographia "Haladás R. T.," 1926.

Sole, Jacobus, *Praelectiones in Lib. V Codicis Iuris Canonici—De Delictis et Poenas,* Romae: Pustet, 1920.

Suarez, Franciscus, *Opera Omnia,* 26 vols., Parisiis, 1856-1866.

Swoboda, Innocent R., *Ignorance in Relation to the Imputability of Delicts,* The Catholic University of America Canon Law Studies, n. 143, Washington, D. C.: The Catholic University of America Press, 1941.

Thomassinus, Ludovicus, *Vetus et Nova Ecclesiae Disciplina circa Beneficia et Beneficiarios, Parisiis,* 1688.

Vermeersch, A.-Creusen, J., *Epitome Iuris Canonici cum Commentariis ad Scholas et ad Usum Privatum,* 3. ed., 3 vols., Mechlinae-Romae: Dessain, 1927-1928.

Wernz, Franciscus X, *Ius Decretalium ad Usum Praelectionum in Scholis Textus Canonici sive Iuris Decretalium,* 6 vols. in 7, Romae-Prati, 1899-1913.

Woywod, Stanislaus, *A Practical Commentary on the Code of Canon Law,* 6. ed., 2 vols., New York: Wagner, 1941.

Zallinger, Jac. Ant., *Institutiones Juris Ecclesiastici,* 9 vols. in 5, Romae, 1823.

Articles

Coucke, V., "De absolutione a peccatis reservatis,"—*Collationes Brugenses,* XXVIII (1928), 233-236.

Creusen, J., "De Reservatione Censurae Praecepto Latae,"—*Jus. Pont.,* IV (1924), 26-29.

———, "La reserve des censures 'ab homine,'"—*NRT,* LV (1928), 436-444.

Darmanin, M., "De Reservatione Peccatorum Iure Codicis Piano-Benedictini,"—*Angelicum,* V (1928), 55-70; 213-241; 539-554.

Kane, T., "Suspension of Faculties from Absolving from Cases Reserved to Ordinaries,"—*AER,* LXXII (1925), 399-402.

Kinane, J., "The Reservation of Censures 'Latae Sententiae' Imposed by a Particular Precept,"—*IER,* XL (1932), 528-534.

Michiels, Gommarus, "De reservatione censurae latae sententiae praecepto peculiari adnexae,"—*ETL,* IV (1927), 180-194; 613-619.

Noval, J., "De Ratione Corregendi et Puniendi sive in Judicio sive extra Jure Codicis Juris Canonici,"—*Jus Pont.,* II (1922), 147-156; III (1923), 36-40; 204-210.

Roberti, Franciscus, "Quaenam Poenae Applicari Possint per Modum Praecepti,"—*Apollinaris,* IV (1931), 297-299.

———, "An censura latae sententiae per praeceptum constituta sit reservata,"—*Apollinaris,* VI (1933), 341-348.

Van Hove, A., "Leges quae ordini publico consulunt,"—*ETL,* I (1924), 153-167.

———, "La territorialité et la personalité de lois en droit canonique depuis Gratien (vers 1140) jusqu'a Jean Andreae (✠ 1348)"—*Tijdschrift voor Rechtsgeschiedenis; Revue d'histoire du droit,* 277-332.

Vermeersch, A., "Annotationes,"—*Periodica,* X (1922), 252-257.

Vitali, I., "De Crimine Occulto Abortus, deque Facultate ab Eodem, Tempore Quoque Iubilaei Maximi, Absolvendi,"—*AER,* LXXIII (1925), 278-284.

———, "Utrum Locorum Ordinarii Valeant Suspendere Privilegium Regularium 'Absolvendi a Casibus Papalibus Ordinariis Reservatis' per Accidens et Via Exceptionis,"—*AER,* LXXXVI (1932), 292-296.

———, "De Reservationibus Pontificiis a Jure Reservatis Ordinario deque Regularium Privilegio ab Iisdem Absolvendi,"—*CpR,* XIV (1933), 287-294; 363-375; 436-447.

———, "Finis Controversiae circa casus a Iure Reservatos,"—*CpRM,* XVI (1935), 164-175.

Anonymous—*AER,* LXVII (1922), 519-522; LXXXV (1931), 75-82; LXXXVI (1932), 297-305.

Anonymous, "Consultationes,"—*Jus Pont.,* XIII (1933), 302.

Anonymous, "Il Codice di Diritto Canonico-Riasunto e Dilucidazioni"—*Il Monitore Ecclesiastico,* Serie IV, Vol. IV, Vol. XXXIV of Collection (1922), 146-149.

Periodicals

Apollinaris, Romae, 1928-

Collationes Brugenses, Brugis Flandorum, 1896-

Commentarium pro Religiosis, Romae, 1920-; ab anno 1935 *Commentarium pro Religiosis et Missionariis.*

Ecclesiastical Review, The (originally *The American Ecclesiastical Review*), Philadelphia, 1889-; *The American Ecclesiastical Review,* 1944-

Ephemerides Theologicae Lovanienses, Brugis, 1924-

Irish Ecclesiastical Record, The, Dublin, 1864-
Jus Pontificium, Romae, 1921-
Monitore Ecclesiastico, Il, Romae, 1876-
Nouvelle Revue Théologique, Paris, 1869-
Periodica de Re Canonica et Morali utili Praesertim Religiosis et Missionariis, Bruges, 1905-
Tijdschrift voor Rechtsgeschiedenis, Revue d'histoire du Droit, Haarlem, 1918-
Unio Thomistica, Romae, 1924- ; ab anno 1925 *Angelicum.*

ABBREVIATIONS

AAS—Acta Apostolicae Sedis.
AER—American Ecclesiastical Review.
CpR—Commentarium pro Religiosis.
CpRM—Commentarium Pro Religiosis et Missionariis.
ETL—Ephemerides Theologicae Lovanienses.
Fontes—Codicis Iuris Canonici Fontes cura . . . Gasparri editi.
IER—Irish Ecclesiastical Review.
JE—Jaffé, *Regesta Pontificum Romanorum*—section edited by Ewald.
JK—Jaffé, *Regesta Pontificum Romanorum*—section edited by Kaltenbrunner.
JL—Jaffé, *Regesta Pontificum Romanorum*—section edited by Löwenfeld.
Jus Pont.-Jus Pontificium.
NRT—Nouvelle Revue Théologique.
Periodica—Periodica de Re Canonica et Morali Utili praesertim Religiosis et Missionariis.
Potthast—*Regesta Pontificum Romanorum.*

ALPHABETICAL INDEX

BIOGRAPHICAL NOTE

Casimir Joseph Stadalnikas was born on January 8, 1917, at Philadelphia, Pennsylvania. He attended the parochial schools of St. Augustine and of St. Andrew. In 1933 he was graduated from St. Joseph's Preparatory High School at Philadelphia and studied at Marianapolis College, Thompson, Connecticut. In 1934 he entered the Novitiate of Marian Fathers at Hinsdale, Illinois, and was professed on July 16, 1935. After his philosophical and theological studies at Marian Seminary, Hinsdale, Illinois, he was ordained to the priesthood on May 26, 1940. After he had completed his final year of theology in 1941, he was sent by his Superior to the Catholic University of America, from which he received the Baccalaureate Degree in Canon Law in May, 1942, and the Licentiate Degree in May, 1943.

CANON LAW STUDIES*

1. Freriks, Rev. Celestine A., C.PP.S., J.C.D., Religious Congregations in Their External Relations, 121 pp., 1916.
2. Galliher, Rev. Daniel M., O.P., J.C.D., Canonical Elections, 117 pp., 1917.
3. Borkowski, Rev. Aurelius L., O.F.M., J.C.D., De Confraternitatibus Ecclesiasticis, 136 pp., 1918.
4. Castillo, Rev. Cayo, J.C.D., Disertacion Historico-Canonica sobre la Potestad del Cabildo en Sede Vacante o Impedida del Vicario Capitular, 99 pp., 1919 (1918).
5. Kubelbeck, Rev. William J., S.T.B., J.C.D., The Sacred Penitentiaria and Its Relation to Faculties of Ordinaries and Priests, 129 pp., 1918.
6. Petrovits, Rev. Joseph J. C., S.T.D., J.C.D., The New Church Law on Matrimony, X-461 pp., 1919.
7. Hickey, Rev. John J., S.T.B., J.C.D., Irregularities and Simple Impediments in the New Code of Canon Law, 100 pp., 1920.
8. Klekotka, Rev. Peter J., S.T.B., J.C.D., Diocesan Consultors, 179 pp., 1920.
9. Wanenmacher, Rev. Francis, J.C.D., The Evidence in Ecclesiastical Procedure Affecting the Marriage Bond, 1920 (Printed 1935).
10. Golden, Rev. Henry Francis, J.C.D., Parochial Benefices in the New Code, IV-119 pp., 1921 (Printed 1925).
11. Koudelka, Rev. Charles J., J.C.D., Pastors, Their Rights and Duties According to the New Code of Canon Law, 211 pp., 1921.
12. Melo, Rev. Antonius, O.F.M., J.C.D., De Exemptione Regularium, X-188 pp., 1921.
13. Schaaf, Rev. Valentine Theodore, O.F.M., S.T.B., J.C.D., The Cloister, X-180 pp., 1921.
14. Burke, Rev. Thomas Joseph, S.T.D., J.C.D., Competence in Ecclesiastical Tribunals, IV-117 pp., 1922.
15. Leech, Rev. George Leo, J.C.D., A Comparative Study of the Constitution "Apostolicae Sedis" and the "Codex Juris Canonici," 179 pp., 1922.
16. Motry, Rev. Hubert Louis, S.T.D., J.C.D., Diocesan Faculties According to the Code of Canon Law, II-167 pp., 1922.
17. Murphy, Rev. George Lawrence, J.C.D., Delinquencies and Penalties in the Administration and the Reception of the Sacraments, IV-121 pp., 1923.

* Below n. 100 only the following numbers are still available: Nn. 3, 4, 9, 25, 34, 57 and 75. Beginning with n. 100 only the following are unavailable: Nn. 100-111 inclusive, and n. 113.

18. O'Reilly, Rev. John Anthony, S.T.B., J.C.D., Ecclesiastical Sepulture in the New Code of Canon Law, 11-129 pp., 1923.
19. Michalicka, Rev. Wenceslas Cyril, O.S.B., J.C.D., Judicial Procedure in Dismissal of Clerical Exempt Religious, 107 pp., 1923.
20. Dargin, Rev. Edward Vincent, S.T.B., J.C.D., Reserved Cases According to the Code of Canon Law, IV-103 pp., 1924.
21. Godfrey, Rev. John A., S.T.B., J.C.D., The Right of Patronage According to the Code of Canon Law, 153 pp., 1924.
22. Hagedorn, Rev. Francis Edward, J.C.D., General Legislation on Indulgences, II-154 pp., 1924.
23. King, Rev. James Ignatius, J.C.D., The Administration of the Sacraments to Dying Non-Catholics, V-141 pp., 1924.
24. Winslow, Rev. Francis Joseph, O.F.M., J.C.D., Vicars and Prefects Apostolic, IV-149 pp., 1924.
25. Correa, Rev. Jose Servelion, S.T.L., J.C.D., La Potestad Legislativa de là Iglesia Catolica, IV-127 pp., 1925.
26. Dugan, Rev. Henry Francis, A.M., J.C.D., The Judiciary Department of the Diocesan Curia, 87 pp., 1925.
27. Keller, Rev. Charles Frederick, S.T.B., J.C.D., Mass Stipends, 167 pp., 1925.
28. Paschang, Rev. John Linus, J.C.D., The Sacramentals According to the Code of Canon Law, 129 pp., 1925.
29. Piontek, Rev. Cyrillus, O.F.M., S.T.B., J.C.D., De Indulto Exclaustrationis necnon Saecularizationis, XIII-289 pp., 1925.
30. Kearney, Rev. Richard Joseph, S.T.B., J.C.D., Sponsors at Baptism According to the Code of Canon Law, IV-127 pp., 1925.
31. Bartlett, Rev. Chester Joseph, A.M., LL.B., J.C.D., The Tenure of Parochial Property in the United States of America, V-108 pp., 1926.
32. Kilker, Rev. Adrian Jerome, J.C.D., Extreme Unction, V-425 pp., 1926.
33. McCormick, Rev. Robert Emmett, J.C.D., Confessors of Religious, VIII-266 pp., 1926.
34. Miller, Rev. Newton Thomas, J.C.D., Founded Masses According to the Code of Canon Law, VII-93 pp., 1926.
35. Roelker, Rev. Edward G., S.T.D., J.C.D., Principles of Privilege According to the Code of Canon Law, XI-166 pp., 1926.
36. Bakalarczyk, Rev. Richardus, M.I.C., J.U.D., De Novitiatu, VIII-208 pp., 1927.
37. Pizzuti, Rev. Lawrence, O.F.M., J.U.L., De Parochis Religiosis, 1927. (Not Printed.)
38. Bliley, Rev. Nicholas Martin, O.S.B., J.C.D., Altars According to the Code of Canon Law, XIX-132 pp., 1927.
39. Brown, Mr. Brendan Francis, A.B., LL.M., J.U.D., The Canonical Juristic Personality with Special Reference to its Status in the United States of America, V-212 pp., 1927.

40. Cavanaugh, Rev. William Thomas, C.P., J.U.D., The Reservation of the Blessed Sacrament, VIII-101 pp., 1927.
41. Doheny, Rev. William J., C.S.C., A.B., J.U.D., Church Property: Modes of Acquisition, X-118 pp., 1927.
42. Feldhaus, Rev. Aloysius H., C.PP.S., J.C.D., Oratories, IX-141 pp., 1927.
43. Kelly, Rev. James Patrick, A.B., J.C.D., The Jurisdiction of the Simple Confessor, X-208 pp., 1927.
44. Neuberger, Rev. Nicholas J., J.C.D., Canon 6 or the Relation of the Codex Juris Canonici to the Preceding Legislation, V-95 pp., 1927.
45. O'Keefe, Rev. Gerald Michael, J.C.D., Matrimonial Dispensations, Powers of Bishops, Priests, and Confessors, VIII-232 pp., 1927.
46. Quigley, Rev. Joseph A. M., A.B., J.C.D., Condemned Societies, 139 pp., 1927.
47. Zaplotnik, Rev. Johannes Leo, J.C.D., De Vicariis Foraneis, X-142 pp., 1927.
48. Duskie, Rev. John Aloysius, A.B., J.C.D., The Canonical Status of the Orientals in the United States, VIII-196 pp., 1928.
49. Hyland, Rev. Francis Edward, J.C.D., Excommunication, Its Nature, Historical Development and Effects, VIII-181 pp., 1928.
50. Reinmann, Rev. Gerald Joseph, O.M.C., J.C.D., The Third Order Secular of Saint Francis, 201 pp., 1928.
51. Schenk, Rev. Francis J., J.C.D., The Matrimonial Impediments of Mixed Religion and Disparity of Cult, XVI-318 pp., 1929.
52. Coady, Rev. John Joseph, S.T.D., J.U.D., A.M., The Appointment of Pastors, VIII-150 pp., 1929.
53. Kay, Rev. Thomas Henry, J.C.D., Competence in Matrimonial Procedure, VIII-164 pp., 1929.
54. Turner, Rev. Sidney Joseph, C.P., J.U.D., The Vow of Poverty, XLIX-217 pp., 1929.
55. Kearney, Rev. Raymond A., A.B., S.T.D., J.C.D., The Principles of Delegation, VII-149 pp., 1929.
56. Conran, Rev. Edward James, A.B., J.C.D., The Interdict, V-163 pp., 1930.
57. O'Neill, Rev. William H., J.C.D., Papal Rescripts of Favor, VII-218 pp., 1930.
58. Bastnagel, Rev. Clement Vincent, J.U.D., The Appointment of Parochial Adjutants and Assistants, XV-257 pp., 1930.
59. Ferry, Rev. William A., A.B., J.C.D., Stole Fees, V-136 pp., 1930.
60. Costello, Rev. John Michael, A.B., J.C.D., Domicile and Quasi-Domicile, VII-201 pp., 1930.
61. Kremer, Rev. Michael Nicholas, A.B., S.T.B., J.C.D., Church Support in the United States, VI-136 pp., 1930.
62. Angulo, Rev. Luis, C.M., J.C.D., Legislation de la Iglesia sobre la intencion en la application de la Santa Misa, VII-104 pp., 1931.

63. Frey, Rev. Wolfgang Norbert, O.S.B., A.B., J.C.D., The Act of Religious Profession, VIII-174 pp., 1931.
64. Roberts, Rev. James Brendan, A.B., J.C.D., The Banns of Marriage, XIV-140 pp., 1931.
65. Ryder, Rev. Raymond Aloysius, A.B., J.C.D., Simony, IX-151 pp., 1931.
66. Campagna, Rev. Angelo, Ph.D., J.U.D., Il Vicario Generale del Vescovo, VII-205 pp., 1931.
67. Cox, Rev. Joseph Godfrey, A.B., J.C.D., The Administration of Seminaries, VI-124 pp., 1931.
68. Gregory, Rev. Donald J., J.U.D., The Pauline Privilege, XV-165 pp., 1931.
69. Donohue, Rev. John F., J.C.D., The Impediment of Crime, VII-110 pp., 1931.
70. Dooley, Rev. Eugene A., O.M.I., J.C.D., Church Law on Sacred Relics, IX-143 pp., 1931.
71. Orth, Rev. Clement Raymond, O.M.C., J.C.D., The Approbation of Religious Institutes, 171 pp., 1931.
72. Pernicone, Rev. Joseph M., A.B., J.C.D., The Ecclesiastical Prohibition of Books, XII-267 pp., 1932.
73. Clinton, Rev. Connell, A.B., J.C.D., The Paschal Precept, IX-108 pp., 1932.
74. Donnelly, Rev. Francis B,. A.M., S.T.L., J.C.D., The Diocesan Synod, VIII-125 pp., 1932.
75. Torrente, Rev. Camilo, C.M.F., J.C.D., Las Procesiones Sagradas, V-145 pp., 1932.
76. Murphy, Rev. Edwin J., C.PP.S., J.C.D., Suspension Ex Informata Conscientia, XI-122 pp., 1932.
77. MacKenzie, Rev. Eric F., A.M., S.T.L., J.C.D., The Delict of Heresy in its Commission, Penalization, Absolution, VII-124 pp., 1932.
78. Lyons, Rev. Avitus E., S.T.B., J.C.D., The Collegiate Tribunal of First Instance, XI-147 pp., 1932.
79. Connolly, Rev. Thomas A., J.C.D., Appeals, XI-195 pp., 1932.
80. Sangmeister, Rev. Joseph V., A.B., J.C.D., Force and Fear as Precluding Matrimonial Consent, V-211 pp., 1932.
81. Jaeger, Rev. Leo A., A.B., J.C.D., The Administration of Vacant and Quasi-Vacant Episcopal Sees in the United States, IX-229 pp., 1932.
82. Rimlinger, Rev. Herbert T., J.C.D., Error Invalidating Matrimonial Consent, VII-79 pp., 1932.
83. Barrett, Rev. John D. M., S.S., J.C.D., A Comparative Study of the Third Plenary Council of Baltimore and the Code, IX-221 pp., 1932.
84. Carberry, Rev. John J., Ph.D., S.T.D., J.C.D., The Juridical Form of Marriage, X-177 pp., 1934.
85. Dolan, Rev. John L., A.B., J.C.D., The Defensor Vinculi, XII-157 pp., 1934.

86. Hannan, Rev. Jerome D., A.M., S.T.D., LL.B., J.C.D., The Canon Law of Wills, IX-517 pp., 1934.
87. Lemieux, Rev. Delise A., A.M., J.C.D., The Sentence in Ecclesiastical Procedure, IX-131 pp., 1934.
88. O'Rourke, Rev. James J., A.B., J.C.D., Parish Registers, VII-109 pp., 1934.
89. Timlin, Rev. Bartholomew, O.F.M., A.M., J.C.D., Conditional Matrimonial Consent, X-381 pp., 1934.
90. Wahl, Rev. Francis X., A.B., J.C.D., The Matrimonial Impediments of Consanguinity and Affinity, VI-125 pp., 1934.
91. White, Rev. Robert J., A.B., LL.B., S.T.B., J.C.D., Canonical Ante-Nuptial Promises and the Civil Law, VI-152 pp., 1934.
92. Herrera, Rev. Antonio Parra, O.C.D., J.C.D., Legislacion Ecclesiastica sobra el Ayuno y la Abstinencia, XI-191 pp., 1935.
93. Kennedy, Rev. Edwin J., J.C.D., The Special Matrimonial Process in Cases of Evident Nullity, X-165 pp., 1935.
94. Manning, Rev. John J., A.B., J.C.D., Presumption of Law in Matrimonial Procedure, XI-111 pp., 1935.
95. Moeder, Rev. John M., J.C.D., The Proper Bishop for Ordination and Dimissorial Letters, VII-135 pp., 1935.
96. O'Mara, Rev. William A., A.B., J.C.D., Canonical Causes for Matrimonial Dispensations, IX-155 pp., 1935.
97. Reilly, Rev. Peter, J.C.D., Residence of Pastors, IX-81 pp., 1935.
98. Smith, Rev. Mariner T., O.P., S.T.Lr., J.C.D., The Penal Law for Religious, VII-169 pp., 1935.
99. Whalen, Rev. Donald W., A.M., J.C.D., The Value of Testimonial Evidence in Matrimonial Procedure, XIII-297 pp., 1935.
100. Cleary, Rev. Joseph F., J.C.D., Canonical Limitations on the Alienation of Church Property, VIII-141 pp., 1936.
101. Glynn, Rev. John C., J.C.D., The Promoter of Justice, XX-337 pp., 1936.
102. Brennan, Rev. James H., S.S., M.A., S.T.B., J.C.D., The Simple Convalidation of Marriage, VI-135 pp., 1937.
103. Bbunini, Rev. Joseph Bernard, J.C.D., The Clerical Obligations of Canons 139 and 142, X-121 pp., 1937.
104. Connor, Rev. Maurice, A.B., J.C.D., The Administrative Removal of Pastors, VIII-159 pp., 1937.
105. Guilfoyle, Rev. Merlin Joseph, J.C.D., Custom, XI-144 pp., 1937.
106. Hughes, Rev. James Austin, A.B., A.M., J.C.D., Witnesses in Criminal Trials of Clerics, IX-140 pp., 1937.
107. Jansen, Rev. Raymond J., A.B., S.T.L., J.C.D., Canonical Provisions for Catechetical Instruction, VII-153 pp., 1937.
108. Kealy, Rev. John James, A.B., J.C.D., The Introductory Libellus in Church Court Procedure, XI-121 pp., 1937.
109. McManus, Rev. James Edward, C.SS.R., J.C.D., The Administration of Temporal Goods in Religious Institutes, XVI-196 pp., 1937.

110. MORIARTY, REV. EUGENE JAMES, J.C.D., Oaths in Ecclesiastical Courts, X-115 pp., 1937.
111. RAINER, REV. ELIGIUS GEORGE, C.SS.R., J.C.D., Suspension of Clerics, XVII-249 pp., 1937.
112. REILLY, REV. THOMAS F., C.SS.R., J.C.D., Visitation of Religious, VI-195 pp., 1938.
113. MORIARITY, REV. FRANCIS E., C.SS.R., J.C.D., The Extraordinary Absolution from Censures, XV-334 pp., 1938.
114. CONNOLLY, REV. NICHOLAS P., J.C.D., The Canonical Erection of Parishes, X-132 pp., 1938.
115. DONOVAN, REV. JAMES JOSEPH, J.C.D., The Pastor's Obligation in Prenuptial Investigation, XII-322 pp., 1938.
116. HARRIGAN, REV. ROBERT J., M.A., S.T.B., J.C.D., The Radical Sanation of Invalid Marriages, VIII-208 pp., 1938.
117. BOFFA, REV. CONRAD HUMBERT, J.C.D., Canonical Provisions for Catholic Schools, VII-211 pp., 1939.
118. PARSONS, REV. ANSCAR JOHN, O.M.Cap., J.C.D., Canonical Elections, XII-236 pp., 1939.
119. REILLY, REV. EDWARD MICHAEL, A.B., J.C.D., The General Norms of Dispensation, XII-156 pp., 1939.
120. RYAN, REV. GERALD ALOYSIUS, A.B., J.C.D., Principles of Episcopal Jurisdiction, XII-172 pp., 1939.
121. BURTON, REV. FRANCIS JAMES, C.S.C., A.B., J.C.D., A Commentary on Canon 1125, X-222 pp., 1940.
122. MIASKIEWICZ, REV. FRANCIS SIGISMUND, J.C.D., Supplied Jurisdiction According to Canon 209, XII-340 pp., 1940.
123. RICE, REV. PATRICK WILLIAM, A.B., J.C.D., Proof of Death in Prenuptial Investigation, VIII-156 pp., 1940.
124. ANGLIN, REV. THOMAS FRANCIS, M.S., J.C.D., The Eucharistic Fast, VIII-183 pp., 1941.
125. COLEMAN, REV. JOHN JEROME, J.C.D., The Minister of Confirmation, VI-153 pp., 1941.
126. DOWNS, REV. JOSEPH EMMANUEL, A.B., J.C.D., The Concept of Clerical Immunity, XI-163 pp., 1941.
127. ESSWEIN, REV. ANTHONY ALBERT, J.C.D., Extrajudicial Penal Powers of Ecclesiastical Superiors, X-144 pp., 1941.
128. FARRELL, REV. BENJAMIN FRANCIS, M.A., S.T.L., J.C.D., The Rights and Duties of the Local Ordinary Regarding Congregations of Women Religious of Pontifical Approval, V-195 pp., 1941.
129. FEENEY, REV. THOMAS JOHN, A.B., S.T.L., J.C.D., Restitutio in Integrum, VI-169 pp., 1941.
130. FINDLAY, REV. STEPHEN WILLIAM, O.S.B., A.B., J.C.D., Canonical Norms Governing the Deposition and Degradation of Clerics, XVII-279 pp., 1941.
131. GOODWINE, REV. JOHN, A.B., S.T.L., J.C.D., The Right of the Church to Acquire Property, VIII-119 pp., 1941.

132. Heston, Rev. Edward Louis, C.S.C., Ph.D., S.T.D., J.C.D., The Alienation of Church Property in the United States, XII-222 pp., 1941.
133. Hogan, Rev. James John, A.B., S.T.L., J.C.D., Judicial Advocates and Procurators, XIII-200 pp., 1941.
134. Kealy, Rev. Thomas M., A.B., Litt.D., J.C.D., Dowry of Women Religious, IX-152 pp., 1941.
135. Keene, Rev. Michael James, O.S.B., J.C.D., Religious Ordinaries and Canon 198, V-164 pp., 1942.
136. Kerin, Rev. Charles A., S.S., M.A., S.T.B., J.C.D., The Privation of Christian Burial, XVI-279 pp., 1941.
137. Louis, Rev. William Francis, M.A., J.C.D., Diocesan Archives, X-101 pp., 1941.
138. McDevitt, Rev. Gilbert Joseph, A.B., J.C.D., Legitimacy and Legitimation, X-247 pp., 1941.
139. McDonough, Rev. Thomas Joseph, A.B., J.C.D., Apostolic Administrators, X-217 pp., 1941.
140. Meier, Rev. Carl Anthony, A.B., J.C.D., Penal Administration Procedure Against Negligent Pastors, XI-240 pp., 1941.
141. Schmidt, Rev. John Rogg, A.B., J.C.D., The Principles of Authentic Interpretation in Canon 17 of the Code of Canon Law, XII-331 pp., 1941.
142. Slafkosky, Rev. Andrew Leonard, A.B., J.C.D., The Canonical Episcopal Visitation of the Diocese, X-197 pp., 1941.
143. Swoboda, Rev. Innocent Robert, O.F.M., J.C.D., Ignorance in Relation to the Imputability of Delicts, IX-271 pp., 1941.
144. Dubé, Rev. Arthur Joseph, A.B., J.C.D., The General Principles for the Reckoning of Time in Canon Law, VIII-299 pp., 1941.
145. McBride, Rev. James T., A.B., J.C.D., Incardination and Excardination of Seculars, XX-585 pp., 1941.
146. Krol, Rev. John T., J.C.D., The Defendant in Ecclesiastical Trials, XII-207 pp., 1942.
147. Comyns, Rev. Joseph J., C.SS.R., A.B., J.C.D., Papal and Episcopal Administration of Church Property, XIV-155 pp., 1942.
148. Barry, Rev. Garrett Francis, O.M.I., J.C.D., Violation of the Cloister, XII-260 pp., 1942.
149. Bolduc, Rev. Gatien, C.S.V., A.B., S.T.L., J.C.D., Les Études dans les Religions Cléricales, VIII-155 pp., 1942.
150. Boyle, Rev. David John, M.A., J.C.D., The Juridic Effects of Moral Certitude on Pre-Nuptial Guarantees, XII-188 pp., 1942.
151. Canavan, Rev. Walter Joseph, M.A., Litt.D., J.C.D., The Profession of Faith, XII-143 pp., 1942.
152. Desrochers, Rev. Bruno, A.B., Ph.L., S.T.B., J.C.D., Le Premier Concile Plénier de Québec et le Code de Droit Canonique, XIV-186 pp., 1942.

153. DILLON, REV. ROBERT EDWARD, A.B., J.C.D., Common Law Marriage, X-148 pp., 1942.
154. DODWELL, REV. EDWARD JOHN, PH.D., S.T.B., J.C.D., The Time and Place for the Celebration of Marriage, X-156 pp., 1942.
155. DONNELLAN, REV. THOMAS ANDREW, A.B., J.C.D., The Obligation of the Misa pro Populo, VII-131 pp., 1942.
156. ELTZ, REV. LOUIS ANTHONY, A.B., J.C.L., Cooperation in Crime.
157. GASS, REV. SYLVESTER FRANCIS, M.A., J.C.D., Ecclesiastical Pensions, XI-206 pp., 1942.
158. GUINIVEN, REV. JOHN JOSEPH, C.SS.R., J.C.D., The Precept of Hearing Mass, XIV-188 pp., 1942.
159. GULCZYNSKI, REV. JOHN THEOPHILUS, J.C.D., The Desecration and Violation of Churches, X-126 pp., 1942.
160. HAMMILL, REV. JOHN LEO, M.A., J.C.D., The Obligations of the Traveler According to Canon 14, VIII-204 pp., 1942.
161. HAYDT, REV. JOHN JOSEPH, A.B., J.C.D., Reserved Benefices, XI-148 pp., 1942.
162. HUSER, REV. ROGER JOHN, O.F.M., A.B., J.C.D., The Crime of Abortion in Canon Law, XII-187 pp., 1942.
163. KEARNEY, REV. FRANCIS PATRICK, A.B., S.T.L., J.C.L., The Principles of Canon 1127
164. LINAHEN, REV. LEO JAMES, S.T.L., J.C.D., De Absolutione Complicis In Peccato Turpi, 114 pp., 1942.
165. MCCLOSKEY, REV. JOSEPH ALOYSIUS, A.B., J.C.D., The Subject of Ecclesiastical Law According to Canon 12, XVII-246 pp., 1942.
166. O'NEILL, REV. FRANCIS JOSEPH, C.SS.R., J.C.D., The Dismissal of Religious in Temporary Vows, XIII-220 pp., 1942.
167. PRINCE, REV. JOHN EDWARD, A.B., S.T.D., J.C.D., The Diocesan Chancellor, X-136 pp., 1942.
168. RIESNER, REV. ALBERT JOSEPH, C.SS.R., J.C.D., Apostates and Fugitives from Religious Institutes, IX-168 pp., 1942.
169. STENGER, REV. JOSEPH BERNARD, J.C.D., The Mortgaging of Church Property, 186 pp., 1942.
170. WALDRON, REV. JOSEPH FRANCIS, A.B., J.C.D., The Minister of Baptism, XII-197 pp., 1942.
171. WILLETT, REV. ROBERT ALBERT, J.C.D., The Probative Value of Documents in Ecclesiastical Trials, X-124 pp., 1942.
172. WOEBER, REV. EDWARD MARTIN, M.A., J.C.D., The Interpellations, XII-161 pp., 1942.
173. BENKO, REV. MATTHEW ALOYSIUS, O.S.B., M.A., J.C.L., The Abbot *Nullius*.
174. CHRIST, REV. JOSEPH JAMES, M.A., S.T.L., J.C.L., Dispensation from Vindicative Penalties.
175. CLANCY, REV. PATRICK M. J., O.P., A.B., S.T.LR., J.C.D., The Local Religious Superior, X-299 pp., 1943.

176. Clarke, Rev. Thomas James, J.C.D., Parish Societies, XII-147 pp., 1943.
177. Connolly, Rev. John Patrick, S.T.L., J.C.D., Synodal Examiners and Parish Priest Consultors, X-223 pp., 1943.
178. Drumm, Rev. William Martin, A.B., J.C.L., Hospital Chaplains.
179. Flanagan, Rev. Bernard Joseph, A.B., S.T.L., J.C.D., The Canonical Erection of Religious Houses, X-147 pp., 1943.
180. Kelleher, Rev. Stephen Joseph, A.B., S.T.B., J.C.D., Discussions with non-Catholics: Canonical Legislation, X-93 pp., 1943.
181. Lewis, Rev. Gordian, C.P., J.C.D., Chapters in Religious Institutes, XII-169 pp., 1943.
182. Marx, Rev. Adolph, J.C.D., The Declaration of Nullity of Marriages Contracted Outside the Church, X-151 pp., 1943.
183. Matulenas, Rev. Raymond Anthony, O.S.B., A.B., J.C.L., Communication, a Source of Privileges.
184. O'Leary, Rev. Charles Gerard, C.SS.R., J.C.D., Religious Dismissed After Perpetual Profession, X-213 pp., 1943.
185. Power, Rev. Cornelius Michael, J.C.L., The Blessing of Cemeteries.
186. Shuhler, Rev. Ralph Vincent, O.S.A., J.C.D., Privileges of Regulars to Absolve and Dispense, XII-195 pp., 1943.
187. Ziolkowski, Rev. Thaddeus Stanislaus, A.B., J.C.D., The Consecration and Blessing of Churches, XII-151 pp., 1943.
188. Heneghan, Rev. John Joseph, S.T.D., J.C.L., The Marriages of Unworthy Catholics: Canons 1065 and 1066.
189. Carroll, Rev. Coleman Francis, M.A., S.T.L., J.C.L., Charitable Institutions.
190. Cieslük, Rev. Joseph Edward, Ph.B., S.T.L., J.C.L., National Parishes in the United States.
191. Coburn, Rev. Vincent Paul, A.B., J.C.L., Marriages of Conscience.
192. Connors, Rev. Charles Paul, C.S.Sp., A.B., J.C.L., Extra-Judicial Procurators in the Code of Canon Law.
193. Coyle, Rev. Paul Raymond, A.B., J.C.L., Judicial Exceptions.
194. Fair, Rev. Bartholomew Francis, A.B., S.T.L., J.C.L., The Impediment of Abduction.
195. Gallagher, Rev. Thomas Raphael, O.P., A.B., S.T.Lr., J.C.L., The Examination of the Qualities of the Ordinand.
196. Gannon, Rev. John Mark, S.T.L., J.C.L., The Interstices Required for the Promotion to Orders.
197. Goldsmith, Rev. J. William, B.C.S., S.T.L., J.C.L., The Competence of Church and State over Marriage—Disputed Points.
198. Goodwine, Rev. Joseph Gerard, A.B., S.T.B., J.C.L., The Reception of Converts.
199. Kowalski, Rev. Romuald Eugene, O.F.M., A.B., J.C.L., Sustenance of Religious Houses of Regulars.
200. McCoy, Rev. Alan Edward, O.F.M., J.C.L., Force and Fear in Relation to Delictual Imputability and Penal Responsibility.

201. McDEVITT, REV. VINCENT JOHN, Ph.B., S.T.L., J.C.L., Perjury.
202. MARTIN, REV. THOMAS OWEN, Ph.D., S.T.D., J.C.L., Adverse Possession, Prescription and Limitation of Actions: The Canonical "Praescriptio."
203. MIKLOSOVIC, REV. PAUL JOHN, A.B., J.C.L., Attempted Marriages and Their Consequent Juridic Effects.
204. MUNDY, REV. THOMAS MAURICE, A.B., S.T.L., J.C.L., The Union of Parishes.
205. O'DEA, REV. JOHN COYLE, A.B., J.C.L., The Matrimonial Impediment of Nonage.
206. OLALIA, REV. ALEXANDER AYSON, S.T.L., J.C.L., A Comparative Study of the Christian Constitution of States and the Constitution of the Philippine Commonwealth.
207. POISSON, REV. PIERRE-MARIE, C.S.C., A.B., Ph.L., Th.L., J.C.L., Droits Patrimoniaux des Maisons et des Eglises Religieuses.
208. STADALNIKAS, REV. CASIMIR JOSEPH, M.I.C., J.C.L., Reservation of Censures.
209. SULLIVAN, REV. EUGENE HENRY, S.T.L., J.C.L., Proof of the Reception of the Sacraments.
210. VAUGHAN, REV. WILLIAM EDWARD, J.C.L., Constitutions for Diocesan Courts.
211. LYONS, REV. JOSEPH HENRY, J.C.L., The Joinder of Issue in Canonical Trials.

www.ingramcontent.com/pod-product-compliance
Lightning Source LLC
LaVergne TN
LVHW050212080826
844660LV00012B/401

* 9 7 8 0 8 1 3 2 2 3 9 2 6 *